Discover Dinnertime

Your guide to building family time around the table

Susan Dosier and Julia Dowling Rutland

Susan Dosier and Julia Dowling Rutland: Authors
Robin Richards: Cover and Book Design

Copyright © 1998 by Susan Dosier and Julia Dowling Rutland

Discoverdinnertime.com

Published by

TRADERY
H·O·U·S·E

Memphis, TN 38118
1-800-548-2537

Library of Congress Cataloging-in-Publication Data
Dosier, Susan.
    Discover Dinnertime: your guide to building family time around the
table/Susan Dosier and Julia Dowling Rutland.
        p. cm.
    Includes index.
    ISBN 1-879958-32-5 (alk. paper)
    1. Cookery. 2. Dinners and dining. I. Rutland, Julia Dowling.
II. Title.
TX714.D677   1998   98-45134
641.5'4--dc21   CIP

First Printing	1998	10,000
Second Printing	1999	10,000
Third Printing	2000	10,000

Printed in the USA by
WIMMER
The Wimmer Companies
Memphis
1-800-548-2537

www.wimmerco.com

Acknowledgments

Some authors liken the completion of a cookbook to the birth of a child. For us, that analogy is especially relevant. Julia was pregnant for the majority of the testing on this book, and Susan tested recipes with two little ones under the age of two underfoot...

Therefore, our thanks to spouses Dit Rutland and Des Keller carries special weight. Without you, we could not have made so many messes, fed you so many weird meals, or sent you to the grocery store so many times. Thanks for babysitting and for logging lots of miles.

We'd also like to thank Glen Wimmer, former president of The Wimmer Companies, whose vision brought the two of us together for this project. Glen, we hope you're as proud of the end result as we are.

We couldn't have completed the book without helpers whose "real life" testing kept us on track: Ruthann Betz-Essinger, Jane Cairns, Margaret Cox, and Lois Edwards, Mary Gunderson, Laura Martin, and Susan's mom, Helen Dosier. A big thank-you goes to Dawn Pradat Cannon for her copy editing.

It's impossible to think about our food influences without acknowledging the *Southern Living* team who over the years expanded our knowledge, encouraged us to grow, and gave us wings. Thank you.

Appreciation goes to the researchers and publications which supplied information for us, including **USA TODAY**, *Child* magazine, *A Cook's Alphabet of Quotations* by Maria Polushkin Robbins, Barbara Fiese, Ph. D., Tony Jurich, Ph. D. and Professor Stephanie Coontz.

And lastly, we thank you. We hope the pages of this cookbook end up splattered with all kinds of good things.

Table of Contents

WELCOME!

Thanks for picking up a copy of our book! In your hands, you hold a guide to improving communication in your family and making supper fun.

Use it and let us know what happens.

The Discover Dinnertime© concept was born out of The Wimmer Companies' commitment to marketing regional cookbooks from Junior Leagues, churches, and civic groups across the country. Those books captured the essence of FAMILY cooking—and the favorite recipes that have been the backbone of the dinner table for years.

From our first meeting with publisher Glen Wimmer, we knew something special was about to happen. For years, Glen had been collecting tips on how to bring families together at the table. Susan was talking about the resurgence of the family dinner hour in trend speeches she was doing across the country. Julia was marketing cookbooks for Wimmer, yet nothing filled this special niche.

And so we bring you this book. One part good recipes, one part inspiration, and one part pure determination. (This book survived one birth, one pregnancy, and lots of other "everyday" family challenges, including flooding basements, tornadoes, and hectic work and business travel schedules. Sound familiar?)

Here, we offer hints, tips, tricks, and recipes gleaned from more than 20 combined years of experience in the food business—and cooking at home.

We really want for you to cook out of this book and let us know what you think. E-mail Susan at sdosier@aol.com and Julia at jrutland@midsouth.rr.com. We invite you to send us your favorite recipes—and YOUR tips for improving dinnertime. Every idea provides inspiration for all of us.

What this book ISN'T about:

GUILT — and feeling guilty about going to restaurants and eating takeout food. More than 60% of the food dollar spent today is spent on food prepared outside the home. Eating out and enjoying take out are part of life. Our goal is to help you on those days you decide to cook at home—to make it easy, fun, and enjoyable. And on those days you do dine out, you can still use our handy tips and conversation starters so that your family gets valuable time together—wherever you lay your napkin.

GOURMET COOKING — we love to cook and eat. These recipes reflect that heartfelt passion. But this book isn't about impressing your friends or ending up on the cover of a food magazine, even though we think that would be fun. This book is about simple techniques, every-day ingredients, and great tasting outcomes.

What this book IS about:

FUN — having fun cooking, getting your family in the kitchen with you, and planning meals so you can happily anticipate coming home to the kitchen; it's about talking with your family at the table and forging new relationships.

FLAVOR — getting the most out of convenience products as well as fresh ingredients. Our volunteer testers said these recipes had a certain personality all their own. We were excited by that comment. Some of these recipes are adventurous while others simply revisit old-fashioned favorites and give them a hearty flavor update.

FAMILY TIME — in the pages that follow, you'll meet moms and dads and husbands and wives, who, like you, struggle with meal planning and cooking. You'll hear their solutions, laugh along with them, and learn along with us. We'll also offer plenty of tips, conversation starters, and helpful ideas adaptable to your family's age and interests. Come on. Let's eat!

Eight Good Reasons To Eat Dinner With Your Family

1. YOUR CHILD WILL READ BETTER:

A 1996 issue of *Child* magazine reported on an 8-year study with principal investigator Catherine Snow, Ph.D., professor of education at Harvard's Graduate School of Education. The study showed that in the 65 families studied over an 8-year period, family dinners (compared to situations such as playtime, school, storytime) offered more opportunities for children to learn vocabulary building words...words that help children read well when children reach third or fourth grade.

2. GOOD CONVERSATION SHAPES THE FUTURE OF OUR COUNTRY.

It's happened to more than one president. The Kennedy children were expected by their parents to come to the table every night and report on one current event. Teddy Roosevelt grew up listening to lively dinner discussions at his family's mealtime. Those conversations reportedly developed his passion for public affairs.

3. SHARED MEALTIMES GIVE YOUR FAMILY A UNIQUE IDENTITY.

Barbara Fiese, Ph.D., a Syracuse University researcher and psychologist reports, "Mealtimes provide an opportunity for families to gather together as a group and develop a sense of belonging with each other. The images of family mealtimes may be passed down across generations and may represent what it means to be a member of MY family."

4. EATING TOGETHER MAY REDUCE CHILDREN'S BEHAVIORAL PROBLEMS.

Fiese's research also shows that families who engage in meaningful mealtimes have children with fewer behavioral problems than families who do not enjoy a positive time together.

Eating breakfast makes a difference, too. A Harvard Medical School/Massachusetts General Hospital study showed that after a free breakfast program was initiated in three Northeastern public schools, the number of students eating breakfast nearly doubled, and reports on the students indicated they were more attentive in the classroom, earned higher grades in math, and had significantly fewer behavioral and emotional problems.

5. TABLE TIME GIVES YOUR CHILDREN A REGULAR TIME TO TALK TO YOU—AND YOU TO THEM.

You may be surprised at what you hear when you regularly ask, "So how was YOUR day?" Consider taking your children (and spouse!) out to dinner one-on-one, occasionally, too. One parent we know picked up valuable insight from his oldest sibling on their "night out." The older child shared his thoughts on difficulties the younger sibling was having at school. Dad listened, and used the information to make positive changes.

Kids — of all ages — can count on this regular time together, giving them an important sense of security and a time to check in at the home front. This may be particularly important as children become more independent and have more demanding schedules.

6. YOU'RE LIKELY TO EAT MORE NUTRITIOUS MEALS WHEN YOU EAT WITH SOMEONE ELSE.

Do you remember the "It's just me—I'll have popcorn and soda for dinner" stage? If you add the kids, your spouse, or a dinner guest, the menu likely takes on a different look. Maybe a few more vegetables or fruits? Maybe a fresh salad along with the take-out food, or something grilled? Healthy doesn't have to be hard, and it tastes better than popcorn.

7. PREPARING MEALS TOGETHER TEACHES YOUR KIDS TO COOK…AND CLEAN UP.

Cooking may open the doors to an exciting culinary career, or simply free them from years of eating peanut butter and jelly once they're independent. The best bonus is additional time to chat. Some parents find more substantial communication occurs while scrubbing potatoes or washing up the dishes than at the table. Even four-year-olds beam with pride when they clear dishes from the table and "help out."

8. THERE'S NO BETTER TIME OR PLACE TO TEACH GOOD MANNERS.

And learn rules of social interaction, and basic consideration for others. Be careful not to turn your table into a battleground or site for the latest power struggle, however. (We all know it happens sometimes, just don't make it the rule.) Polish your own manners and whatever you do, avoid marital conflict at the table.

So, how do you do it?

No one secret works for every family. And what you do will change as your family changes—it may even change day by day or by the sports season. The following tips may spark helpful ideas.

KIDS IN THE KITCHEN

• Reorganize your kitchen to afford your children an opportunity to help you....both in preparing food and cleaning up. Can they reach the measuring cups? The dish towels? Is there a sturdy step stool nearby? Do you have a bowl that allows your youngest to stir without spilling ingredients all over the counter?

• Purchase a special apron, set of measuring spoons, cups, or other kitchen items just for your child. Put his or her name on them and keep them in a special drawer or basket.

• If your child doesn't enjoy cooking, ask him or her to read to you while you cook.

REALITY CHECK

• Having a meal together takes time. Most likely, it will take time away from another important activity. Be realistic about what you may be giving up to make mealtime a priority.

• Eat out! If you like, stick a few conversation starters in your pocket and try them out in the restaurant. Or take advantage of take-out food or frozen meals. You may have time to light a candle, stick a flower in a bud vase, or serve on bright paper plates. Any meal can be special, even if it's not homemade.

SMART COOKIES

• In the Ken Doyle family of Gillespie, Illinois, everyone has an assigned weeknight to cook, including Ken and his two teenage sons. We asked Ken how he got his sons to cook. He answered with this story.

When a young 4-H exchange student from another country stayed with the family, he vowed he wouldn't cook, saying it was woman's work. Ken answered him simply, "You don't cook, you don't eat." The young man cooked. And so do Ken's sons.

• Find a day of the week or month that can be identified as a special mealtime. This can range from Friday pizza night to celebrating the first Sunday of the month with a candlelight supper. In Leland, Mississippi, Kiki Stovall and her family enjoy a 25-year tradition of hamburgers on Friday night.

• In Birmingham, Alabama, super mom Mandy Rogers manages a household and five children, ages 10, 8, and 4 (the four-year-olds are triplets). This family enjoys theme dinners. The rules are simple. She fixes whatever dish the children request, and they do the rest, decorating or dressing up for the evening.

The triplets recently planned a Dalmation Dinner where they cut out black construction paper "spots" and taped them to a white tablecloth, and the children made a centerpiece for the table with dog bones. Dessert continued the black and white theme, featuring vanilla ice cream with the instant chocolate shell coating.

Mandy's son's favorite theme night was a dinner/dance, featuring fettuccine alfredo by candlelight. The dress code was suits (Dad even wore his tuxedo) and party dresses. After dinner entertainment included dancing to her son's musical selections.

START A SUPPER CO-OP

• Start a supper co-op. Gather three to four families or individuals, with similar food preferences or lifestyles. Each family selects a night and prepares supper for themselves and the other families. It can be as simple as preparing hamburgers or a one-dish meal. After your cooking "shift", take the other nights off as the other families take their turns.

At your co-op planning meeting, jot down who will be cooking and the name of the dish for each night on a calendar at least a month in advance. Work out delivery details as a group. You can swap food at the office refrigerator or deliver dishes to homes (or to a cooler on the front steps if the recipients aren't there).

Getting It Done

- Sarah Shelton, an ordained Baptist minister, finds relief by cooking ahead of time. On her day off, she cooks while her kids are at school and freezes dishes for the busy week ahead.

- Consider posting a weekly calendar with each night's menu on your refrigerator. Spell out what your kitchen helpers can do if they're home before you are.

- Select a few easy recipes from this book and keep the ingredient lists on cards in your wallet so you can stop by the supermarket on your way home. Fall back on these favorites when you're shortest on time.

- Whenever possible, unplug the phone during the dinner hour, or let the answering machine pick up calls.

You Can Overdo It...

Don't get too hung up on a rigid dinner situation where everyone feels forced to talk, says author Stephanie Coontz, a family studies professor at Evergreen State College in Olympia, Washington.

Good talk time with your teen may include late-night munchies with a video or sharing a pizza in front of the television. (The television? Gasp!)

Coontz says the point is to find time to be with members of your family. Don't torture teens with an inflexible routine. If dinnertime becomes a family issue, the practice may offer more harm than benefits. Teens often talk more if they're involved in an alternative activity than if the focus is specifically on them.

Helpful Symbols In This Book

 Quick: Ready in 30 minutes, start to finish

 Kid Friendly: Taste tested and approved by kids

 Heart Healthy: Lower in calories and fat; recipes have 30 to 35 percent calories from fat. Nutritional data from commercial products varies by brand; values are approximate.

Pasta

Everything you see,
I owe to spaghetti.

Sophia Loren

Conversation Starters

- ## CENTERPIECE SENSATIONS
Assign each member of the family a day (or week) to be in charge of the centerpiece. Flowers aren't the only option—consider a favorite toy, the latest art project, sports equipment, a book. You get the idea.

- ## PLAN A PICNIC
Ask your family to serve their plates from the oven or cooktop, and then go outside to eat. Raining? Spread a quilt on the living room floor.

- ## MAGIC PORTION
Let the kids serve the plates tonight, and enjoy their version of portion control.

Bow Tie Pasta with Artichoke Hearts, Tomatoes, and Capers

2 tablespoons olive oil
1 onion, halved and sliced
2 cloves garlic, minced
1 (6-ounce) jar marinated artichoke
   hearts, undrained
1 (14.5-ounce) can diced tomatoes
1 teaspoon capers
8 ounces uncooked bow tie pasta
¼ cup freshly grated Parmesan cheese

Heat oil in a large skillet over medium-high heat until hot. Add onion and garlic; cook 3 to 5 minutes or until tender. Stir in artichoke hearts, tomatoes, and capers.

Meanwhile, cook pasta according to package directions omitting salt and fat; drain.

Toss pasta with sauce, and sprinkle with cheese.

Yield: 4 servings.

Some pasta lovers prefer their noodles "al dente" (Italian for "to the tooth"). One test for this degree of doneness is tossing a piece of pasta against your kitchen wall. If it sticks, it's ready. We prefer using a handy timer—or simply taking a bite.

Powder Keg Pasta

This recipe earns its name from the use of chili powder, which lends it a warm, well-rounded flavor. To experience the "keg" part of the title, add heat with the jalapeño peppers or hot sauce.

8 ounces uncooked wagon wheel pasta or spaghetti
1 (16-ounce) can chili hot beans, drained
1 (14.5-ounce) can diced tomatoes with roasted garlic
1 green bell pepper, cut into thin strips
1 fresh jalapeño, seeded and chopped
1 clove garlic, minced
¼ cup olive oil
2 tablespoons fresh lime juice
1 teaspoon chili powder
Monterey Jack cheese, shredded (optional)

Cook pasta according to package directions omitting salt and fat; drain.

Meanwhile, combine beans, tomatoes, bell pepper, jalapeño, garlic, olive oil, lime juice, and chili powder in a large bowl.

Stir in hot cooked pasta. Sprinkle with Monterey Jack cheese, if desired, and serve immediately.

Yield: 4 servings.

Note: To serve children, omit jalapeño.

If you leave the seeds in jalapeño peppers, the little green bombs blast you with even more heat; the ribs also add to the fiery flavor. To tone down the heat and still get the jalapeño flavor, remove seeds and ribs. Be sure to handle the pepper with gloves on, or wash your hands immediately after chopping it. Don't touch your face or rub your eyes.

Pasta with Caramelized Vidalias and Blue Cheese

8 ounces uncooked rotini (twists) pasta
1 slice bacon
3 tablespoons chopped pecans
1 cup fat-free chicken broth, divided
1 Vidalia or other sweet onion, halved
     and sliced
1 teaspoon sugar
2 teaspoons all-purpose flour
1 (5-ounce) can evaporated skimmed milk
¼ cup crumbled blue cheese

If you like blue cheese, you'll love the combination of flavors in this rich, yet low-fat, recipe.

Cook pasta according to package directions omitting salt and fat; drain.

Meanwhile, cook bacon in a nonstick skillet over medium-high heat until crisp. Remove bacon from skillet; crumble and set aside. Reduce heat to medium. Add pecans to bacon fat in skillet; cook 2 minutes or until pecans are toasted, stirring constantly. Remove from skillet, and set aside.

Add ½ cup broth to skillet; bring to a boil. Add onion and sugar. Cook 10 minutes or until onions are golden, stirring frequently.

Place flour in a small bowl; gradually add remaining ½ cup broth and milk, stirring with a whisk until blended. Add flour mixture to onion mixture; cook until slightly thick. Combine onion mixture, pasta, blue cheese, and reserved bacon and pecans; toss gently to coat. Serve immediately.

Yield: 4 servings.

Note: To reduce calories and fat, we replaced butter with chicken broth to "caramelize" the onions.

Per serving: 333 calories, 7.3 g. fat, 8 mg. cholesterol, 300 mg. sodium

Cheese Tortellini with Asparagus

Use this recipe as a basis for other quick pastas. Substitute your favorite cut vegetables for asparagus, and try different refrigerated pastas.

1 (5-ounce) can evaporated skimmed milk
4 ounces (½ cup) Neufchâtel or light cream cheese
1 teaspoon cracked black pepper
1 (9-ounce) package refrigerated cheese-and-herb tortellini
1 pound fresh asparagus, cut into 1-inch pieces

Combine skimmed milk and cream cheese in a small saucepan over medium-low heat. Cook, stirring constantly, until cheese melts and mixture thickens slightly; stir in pepper. Remove from heat.

Cook pasta according to package directions. Three minutes before pasta is done, add cut asparagus to boiling water. Cook 3 minutes or until pasta and asparagus are tender; drain.

Toss pasta and asparagus with sauce. Serve immediately.

Yield: 3 servings.

Salmon and Asparagus Tortellini:
Add 3 ounces sliced smoked salmon when you toss pasta, asparagus, and sauce.

Greek Pasta

Bring the flavors of Greece to the table in about 25 minutes.

8 ounces uncooked penne pasta
1 (14.5-ounce) pasta-style chunky tomatoes
¼ cup white wine
1 (2.25-ounce) can sliced ripe olives, drained
¼ cup olive oil
1 clove garlic, minced
¼-½ cup crumbled feta cheese

Cook pasta according to package directions omitting salt and fat; drain.

Meanwhile, combine tomatoes, wine, and olives in a medium saucepan. Bring to a slow boil over medium heat for 3 to 5 minutes.

Combine olive oil and garlic in a small bowl. Microwave at HIGH 30 seconds.

Place pasta in serving bowl and pour garlicky olive oil over it; toss gently. Add tomato mixture and feta cheese. Stir well, and serve immediately.

Yield: 3 to 4 servings.

Pasta Olé!

To make this pasta a Mexican repast, substitute ½ cup Mexican blend shredded cheese with jalapeño peppers or ½ cup shredded Monterey Jack cheese for the feta cheese.

Did You Know? Authentic Greek feta is a crumbly cheese made from goat or sheep's milk that's pressed into square cakes when it's sold. It boasts a salty, pungent flavor. Look for it alongside other cheeses in the refrigerated section at the supermarket. Some large processors may use cow's milk to make it, and those selections work just fine in this recipe. You may also find it flavored with pepper, sun-dried tomatoes, basil, etc. Those versions work nicely, here, too. Use the leftover feta in casseroles, sandwiches, or other pasta dishes.

Browned Garlic, Tomato, and Basil Pasta

You may use any short, firm pasta for this recipe, but the chunky tomato halves serve easier with a pasta that does not come in strands.

8 ounces uncooked rotini pasta (twists) or bow tie pasta
2 tablespoons olive oil
3 cloves garlic, minced
¼ teaspoon crushed red pepper flakes (optional)
1 pint cherry tomatoes, halved
¼ teaspoon salt
¼ cup fresh basil, shredded or chopped
Freshly grated Parmesan cheese

Cook pasta according to package directions omitting salt and fat; drain.

Meanwhile, place oil in a nonstick skillet over medium-high heat. Add garlic and, if desired, pepper flakes. Cook, stirring constantly, until garlic is lightly browned, but not burned.

Add tomatoes; cook 3 to 4 minutes or until thoroughly heated. Stir in salt and basil. Serve over pasta. Sprinkle with Parmesan cheese.

Yield: 3 servings.

Per serving: 417 calories, 2.7 g. fat, 5 mg. cholesterol, 317 mg. sodium

Turkey-Tomato Basil Pasta:

Add 2 cups chopped cooked turkey when you add tomatoes. Reduce heat to medium, and cook 3 to 4 minutes or until thoroughly heated. Stir in salt and basil. Serve over pasta. Sprinkle with Parmesan cheese.

Yield: 4 servings.

Grilled Chicken Linguine

2 boneless chicken breasts
¼ cup fat-free Italian dressing
8 ounces uncooked linguine
1 teaspoon olive oil
1 onion, quartered and sliced
4 cloves garlic, minced
¼ cup dry white wine
4 ounces (½ cup) Neufchâtel light cream cheese
1 (5-ounce) can evaporated skimmed milk
¾ cup shredded fresh Parmesan cheese, divided
½ teaspoon cracked black pepper
1 tablespoon chopped fresh thyme
1 tomato, chopped

Coat chicken breasts in dressing. Grill chicken, without grill lid, over medium heat (300° to 350°) 10 minutes or until done, turning once. Let cool slightly; cut chicken diagonally across grain into thin slices; keep warm.

Cook pasta according to package directions omitting salt and fat; drain.

Meanwhile, heat oil in a nonstick skillet over medium-high heat until hot. Add onion and garlic; cook 5 minutes or until tender. Add wine; cook until liquid evaporates, stirring frequently.

Add cream cheese and milk to skillet; cook over low heat until cheese melts, stirring frequently. Add ½ cup Parmesan cheese, pepper, and chopped fresh thyme.

Combine cheese sauce and pasta; toss well. Top with chicken and tomato. Sprinkle with remaining ¼ cup Parmesan cheese.

Yield: 4 servings.

Per serving: 480 calories, 14.0 g. fat, 60 mg. cholesterol, 688 mg. sodium

Light cream cheese and evaporated skimmed milk team up to thicken this traditional sauce without adding the usual calories and fat.

Penne with Summer Squash and Spinach

8 ounces uncooked penne pasta
½ cup vegetable or chicken broth
1 Vidalia or other sweet onion, sliced
2 cloves garlic, minced
1 (15.5-ounce) can Great Northern beans, rinsed and drained
3 yellow squash, sliced
2 cups fresh trimmed spinach
1 teaspoon chopped fresh rosemary
½ teaspoon salt
½ teaspoon pepper
2 tablespoons grated fresh Romano cheese

Cook pasta according to package directions omitting salt and fat; drain.

Meanwhile, bring vegetable broth to a boil in a large nonstick skillet over medium-high heat. Add onion and garlic, and cook 3 minutes, stirring occasionally. Add beans, yellow squash, spinach, and fresh rosemary; cover and cook 5 minutes or until vegetables are tender, stirring occasionally. Remove from heat; stir in salt and pepper.

Combine vegetable mixture and pasta in a bowl; toss well. Sprinkle with cheese.

Yield: 4 servings.

Note: The beans add protein and fiber to this low-fat dish. You can substitute your favorite bean in this recipe.

Per serving: 380 calories, 2.6 g. fat, 4 mg. cholesterol, 406 mg. sodium

Hurry-Up Beef Stroganoff

1 (12-ounce) package medium egg
   noodles
1 (10-ounce) package frozen broccoli
   florets
1 tablespoon olive oil
1 (1½-pound) boneless sirloin steak, cut
   into ¼-inch slices
1 (10¾-ounce) reduced-fat cream of
   mushroom soup
1 cup light sour cream
3 tablespoons Worcestershire sauce
2 teaspoons Dijon mustard

Cook egg noodles according to package
directions. During last 5 minutes of cooking,
add broccoli, and continue cooking until
noodles and broccoli are tender.

Heat oil in a nonstick skillet over medium-
high heat. Add steak slices and cook 4 minutes
until browned, stirring constantly. Remove
meat and set aside.

Add soup, sour cream, Worcestershire sauce,
and mustard to skillet. Cook 2 minutes over
medium heat, stirring well. (Do not boil.) Stir
steak into sauce.

Toss broccoli mixture with sauce in a large
serving bowl. Serve immediately

Yield: 4 to 6 servings.

Note: To reheat, stir in small amount of milk;
noodles absorb much of the sauce as they cool.

Serve with a green
salad or steamed
carrots and
breadsticks.

Lime Scampi Pasta

Peel the shrimp, and then begin the recipe. Use a good Sauvignon Blanc in this dish, and serve the rest with dinner.

Zest is the grated skin or rind of a lime, lemon, or orange. Grate citrus over wax paper to remove the skin, but don't grate the pithy white part. Let zest stand on wax paper until you're ready to use it.

8 ounces uncooked linguine, spaghetti, or fettuccini
2 large limes
1 cup butter or margarine
¼ cup chopped green onions with tops
4 cloves garlic, crushed
2 pounds medium-size fresh shrimp, peeled and deveined
½ cup dry white wine
¼ teaspoon cayenne pepper
¼ cup chopped fresh Italian Parsley
½ teaspoon salt

Cook pasta according to package directions omitting fat; drain.

Meanwhile, grate the skin of both limes and set aside. Place limes in microwave and microwave at HIGH 30 seconds. Cut limes in half, juice, and set aside.

Melt butter in a large skillet over medium-high heat. Add green onions and garlic. Cook 2 minutes, stirring occasionally, or until tender.

Reduce heat to medium; add shrimp. Cook 3 to 5 minutes, stirring frequently, until shrimp turn pink. Remove shrimp with a slotted spoon, and toss with pasta.

Add wine, lime juice, lime rind, and cayenne pepper to skillet. Simmer 2 minutes. Pour over shrimp.

Add parsley and salt. Toss pasta to coat. Taste for salt and add more if needed. Serve immediately.

Yield: 4 to 6 servings.

Penne Pasta with White Beans and Tomatoes

Cannellini (pronounced Kan-eh-LEE-nee) beans are white Italian kidney beans. Grocery stores stock a variety of canned brands, so if you can't find the exact can size, get something close. This recipe will work just fine.

12 ounces uncooked penne pasta

1 (19-ounce) can cannellini or other white beans, drained

1 (14.5-ounce) can pasta-style chunky tomatoes

1 (16-ounce can) vegetable or fat-free chicken broth

2 teaspoons herbes de Provence

½ teaspoon garlic powder

1 tablespoon olive oil

½ teaspoon salt

½ teaspoon pepper

¼ cup grated Parmesan cheese

Cook pasta according to package directions omitting salt and fat; drain.

Meanwhile, combine beans, tomatoes, broth, herbes de Provence, and garlic powder in a medium-size saucepan. (Nonstick saucepans are especially helpful with thick bean mixtures— use one if you have it.) Cook 10 to 15 minutes, uncovered, over medium heat.

Toss the cooked pasta with olive oil, salt, and pepper. Spoon pasta into soup or pasta bowls, and ladle sauce over the top. Serve with Parmesan cheese.

Yield: 6 servings.

Per serving: 380 calories, 1.5 g. fat, 5 mg. cholesterol, 911 mg. sodium

Did you know you were reading French when you went down the ingredient list? Herbes de Provence literally translates to "herbs from Provence." (Provence is located in Southern France). This blend usually includes basil, fennel seed, lavender, marjoram, rosemary, sage, summer savory, and thyme—the herbs used most often in the region. The seasoning provides a bouquet of nose-tingling herbs with just a flick of the wrist. Use it to enhance vegetables, meats, soups, and other pasta dishes. We warn you—you'll start adding it to everything.

Pasta with Fresh Pesto and Prosciutto

If you're short on time, you can substitute commercial refrigerated pesto for the Fresh Pesto.

8 ounces uncooked fettuccine
¾ cup Fresh Pesto
⅓ cup slivered prosciutto ham or deli ham
¼ cup sliced sun-dried tomatoes
Freshly grated Parmesan cheese

Cook pasta according to package directions omitting salt and fat; drain.

Combine Fresh Pesto, prosciutto, tomatoes, and pasta; toss to coat. Sprinkle with Parmesan cheese.

Yield: 4 servings.

Fresh Pesto:
1 clove garlic
1 cup lightly packed fresh basil
¼ cup pine nuts, pecans, or walnuts
¼ cup olive oil
⅓ cup freshly grated Parmesan cheese
1 teaspoon lemon juice
¼ teaspoon salt

Combine garlic, basil, and nuts in container of food processor; pulse several times until coarsely chopped.

Add oil, cheese, lemon juice, and salt; pulse until finely ground.

Yield: ¾ cup.

Fresh Pesto and Proscuitto Salad:
Substitute orzo for fettuccine, and serve chilled.

Thumbs Up! Ham and Cheese Pasta

kid friendly

16 ounces uncooked spaghetti
1 (10¾-ounce) can Cheddar cheese soup
1 soup can (1⅓ cups) milk
2 tablespoons Worcestershire sauce
½ teaspoon garlic powder
¼ teaspoon pepper
2 cups chopped, cooked ham
1 tablespoon chopped fresh parsley
   (optional)

Cook pasta according to package directions omitting salt and fat; drain.

Meanwhile, combine soup, milk, Worcestershire sauce, garlic powder, and pepper in a large bowl. Stir well. Cover loosely with plastic wrap. Microwave at HIGH 4 to 5 minutes or until hot.

Add hot spaghetti and ham to the cheese mixture, and stir to coat. Add parsley, if desired, and serve.

Yield: 8 servings.

Broccoli-Ham 'N Cheese Pasta:
Cook a 10-ounce package frozen broccoli florets according to package directions. Drain well, and pat with paper towels. Stir into cheese sauce along with spaghetti. Add parsley and serve.

Broccoli-Ham 'N Cheese Casserole:
Follow directions for the broccoli version of the pasta. Pour spaghetti mixture into a lightly greased 11- x 7-inch casserole dish. Sprinkle with 1 cup breadcrumbs and dust lightly with paprika. Sprinkle with additional fresh chopped parsley. Bake at 350° for 30 minutes or until heated through, or microwave for 12 minutes at HIGH, turning once after 6 minutes.

Broccoli-Cheese Casserole:
Simply omit the ham from the casserole above.

> Susan came up with this recipe when she cooked dinner for a new mom. The oldest sibling said he liked it better than macaroni and cheese. You can make this recipe ahead of time or serve it immediately with a salad and garlic bread.

Grilled Vegetable Primavera

For a change of pace, try grilling eggplant slices or halved leeks. Any "grillable" vegetable can be substituted in this recipe—choose your favorites.

8 ounces uncooked Penne pasta
2 yellow squash, halved lengthwise
2 zucchini, halved lengthwise
2 carrots, peeled and quartered
1 sweet onion, quartered and separated
1 red bell pepper, quartered
3 tablespoons reduced-calorie Italian dressing
2 teaspoons all-purpose flour
1 (12-ounce) can evaporated skimmed milk
2 ounces (about ¼ cup) Neufchâtel light cream cheese
¼ cup shredded mozzarella cheese
2 tablespoons grated fresh Parmesan cheese
½ teaspoon salt
¼ teaspoon cracked black pepper

Cook pasta according to package directions omitting salt and fat; drain.

Meanwhile, combine squash, zucchini, carrots, onion, and bell pepper in a large bowl. Toss with dressing.

Grill vegetables over medium-high heat (350° to 400°) 5 to 7 minutes or until tender, turning occasionally (remove vegetables as they cook to avoid burning). Cool slightly; coarsely chop, and set aside.

Place flour in a small saucepan; gradually add milk, stirring until well blended. Cook over medium heat until slightly thick, stirring constantly. Add cheeses, salt, and pepper, stirring with a wire whisk until cheeses melt. Combine cheese sauce, chopped vegetables, and pasta in a bowl; toss gently to coat. Serve immediately.

Yield: 4 servings.

Per serving: 430 calories, 8.4 g. fat, 23 mg. cholesterol, 607 mg. sodium

Beat-The-Clock Spaghetti

You'll find the Italian sausage in links in the fresh meat case, not with cured or smoked sausages. Italian sausage has plenty of flavorful herbs and seasoning built right in. If you've never used it before, you're in for a treat.

8 ounces uncooked spaghetti or fettuccine
1 pound light turkey or Italian sausage
1 (8-ounce) package sliced fresh mushrooms
1 cup shredded carrots
1 (28-ounce) jar garden-style spaghetti sauce

Cook pasta according to package directions omitting salt and fat; drain.

Meanwhile, coat a large nonstick skillet or Dutch oven with vegetable cooking spray. Place on medium-high heat.

Remove the casings from Italian sausage (just cut them with a knife or kitchen scissors and sausage will come out), and crumble sausage into hot pan. Cook, breaking sausage into bite-size pieces with a wooden spoon until meat is no longer pink.

Reduce heat to medium; add mushrooms and carrots. Cook 2 to 3 minutes until vegetables are tender. Stir in sauce and cook until bubbly and heated through. Serve over spaghetti.

Yield: 4 servings.

Note: 1 (6-ounce) can sliced mushrooms, drained, may be substituted for fresh.

Did you know? We could avoid 500,000 cancer deaths in this country each year if every American ate five servings of fruits and vegetables each day. That's right. So sneak those extra vegetables into this speedy sauce.

Zucchini Tetrazzini

Using fresh herbs adds extra vitality to this meatless dish. If you have only dry herbs, 1 teaspoon dried herbs equals 1 tablespoon fresh.

8 ounces thin spaghetti
2 tablespoons olive oil
2 stalks celery, chopped
4 green onions, chopped
1 green bell pepper, chopped
1 clove garlic, minced
4 tomatoes, seeded and chopped
3 zucchini, sliced
1 teaspoon salt
½ teaspoon pepper
1 tablespoon chopped fresh oregano
1 teaspoon chopped fresh thyme
¼ cup freshly grated Parmesan cheese
½ cup mozzarella cheese, divided

Preheat oven to 350°.

Cook pasta according to package directions, omitting salt and fat; drain.

Place oil in a very large skillet or Dutch oven over medium-high heat. Add celery, onions, bell pepper, and garlic; cook 2 minutes, stirring occasionally, or until tender.

Stir in tomatoes, zucchini, salt, pepper, and herbs. Cook, covered, 5 to 7 minutes or until vegetables are tender. Stir together tomato mixture, Parmesan cheese, ¼ cup mozzarella cheese and cooked spaghetti. Place in lightly greased 13 x 9-inch baking dish. Sprinkle with remaining ¼ cup mozzarella cheese.

Bake 30 minutes until heated through.

Yield: 6 servings.

Per serving: 280 calories, 8.0 g. fat, 9 mg. cholesterol, 438 mg. sodium

Skillet Meals

Successful cooks do as little as
possible to achieve whatever
desired results.

Alan Koehler

Conversation Starters

- **DRESS FOR SUCCESS**
  Ask everyone to come to the table wearing a piece of clothing from another member of the family. Can you guess who everyone is?

- **THE OLD SWITCHEROO**
  In a slump? Swap seats. When one family tried this, each person also assumed the identity of the family member who usually occupied that seat. The ways children choose to imitate their parents is, well, enlightening!

- **FAST 'N' FINE**
  On fast-food night, bring dinner home and dine by candlelight. Set the table with fine china—no elbows allowed!

Mexican Beef and Beans

kid friendly

The only thing you'll need to serve with this easy skillet recipe is a green salad. If your family likes bread for sopping up every drop, serve it with cornbread or tortillas.

1 teaspoon olive or vegetable oil
1 green bell pepper, chopped
2 cloves garlic, minced
1 pound lean ground beef
1 (16-ounce) can chili hot beans, undrained
1 (15½-ounce) can golden hominy, drained
1 (4-ounce) can chopped green chiles
2 teaspoons chili powder
1 cup shredded sharp Cheddar cheese
Hot sauce (optional)

Heat olive oil in a large nonstick skillet over medium heat. Add pepper and garlic. Cook 2 minutes, stirring occasionally, until pepper begins to soften.

Push pepper and garlic to the side of the skillet and add ground beef. Brown ground beef in skillet until meat is no longer pink, crumbling with a wooden spoon. Stir in chili beans, hominy, green chiles, and chili powder. Cook 10 minutes over medium heat. Remove from heat; sprinkle with Cheddar cheese. Serve immediately with hot sauce, if desired.

Yield: 4 servings.

Hominy (corn from which the hull and germ have been removed) was given to the American colonists by native Americans. Another food gift was popcorn. Thank you!

Turkey Cutlets with Artichokes and Capers

½ cup flour
¾ teaspoon salt, divided
½ teaspoon pepper
4 (¼-inch thick) turkey cutlets
2 tablespoons butter, divided
2 tablespoons olive oil, divided
¼ cup white wine or chicken broth
1 (14-ounce) can quartered artichoke hearts, rinsed and drained
2 teaspoons capers

Combine flour, ½ teaspoon salt, and pepper in a shallow dish.

Pound turkey cutlets to ⅛-inch thickness; dredge in flour mixture.

Heat 1 tablespoon butter and 1 tablespoon oil over medium-high heat; add 2 cutlets and cook 6 minutes, or until golden brown, turning once. Remove from skillet; keep warm. Repeat with remaining butter, oil, and cutlets.

Add wine to skillet and bring to a boil over medium-high heat, scraping bits from bottom of pan. Stir in artichoke hearts, capers, and remaining ¼ teaspoon salt, stirring until thoroughly heated. Serve over cutlets.

Yield: 4 servings.

Shrimp Creole

2 tablespoons butter or olive oil
1 onion, chopped
3 stalks celery, chopped
2 cloves garlic, minced
1 green bell pepper, chopped
1 (14.5-ounce) can no-salt-added diced tomatoes
1 (8-ounce) can no-salt-added tomato sauce
1 tablespoon Worcestershire sauce
2 teaspoons Cajun Seasoning Blend (page 178)
1 pound medium-size fresh shrimp, peeled and deveined
4 cups hot cooked rice

Melt butter in a large saucepan over medium-high heat; add onion, celery, garlic, and bell pepper. Cook vegetables, stirring constantly, 4 to 5 minutes or until tender.

Stir in tomatoes, tomato sauce, Worcestershire, and Cajun Seasoning Blend. Cook 2 minutes. Stir in shrimp; cook 5 minutes or until shrimp are pink and tender. Serve over hot cooked rice.

Yield: 4 servings.

Per serving: 467 calories, 7.7 g. fat, 190 mg. cholesterol, 477 mg. sodium

Shrimp Creole harkens from the Mississippi-Louisiana Gulf Coast. It starts with the "trinity" of Cajun/Creole cooking—onion, green bell pepper, and garlic. If you don't have our Cajun blend on hand, use 1 teaspoon of commercial Cajun seasoning.

Apple Harvest Skillet with Sweet Pan Juices

1 tablespoon olive oil
1 sweet potato, peeled and cubed
2 medium-size Granny Smith apples, unpeeled and cut into wedges
1 (16-ounce) can fat-free chicken broth
1 (9-ounce) jar mango chutney (about 1 cup)
2 cups cubed cooked turkey
4 cups hot cooked couscous

Heat olive oil in a large nonstick skillet over medium-high heat. Add sweet potato and apples. Cook 5 minutes, stirring constantly, until browned.

Add chicken broth. Bring to a boil; reduce heat, and simmer 5 minutes, uncovered. Stir in chutney and turkey. Cook until heated through (about 5 minutes). Serve over couscous.

Yield: 4 servings.

Note: For speedy cooking, cut up all ingredients and start couscous before you begin this recipe. Delicious with whole wheat couscous or wild rice.

Per serving: 593 calories, 9.3 g. fat, 52 mg. cholesterol, 309 mg. sodium

Mumba Jumba Pork

Keep this list of ingredients in your wallet, so you won't have to think about what to buy when you need a quick meal. Use quick-cooking, boil-in-bag rice; it's done as quickly as the spicy-sweet meat topping.

4 (1-inch-thick) boneless pork loin
  chops
2½ tablespoons Mexican Seasoning Blend
  (page 178)
1 tablespoon olive or vegetable oil
2 cups salsa
1 (12-ounce) jar apricot preserves
1 (8-ounce) can crushed pineapple,
  undrained
4 cups hot cooked rice

Cut pork into 1-inch cubes; toss with seasoning blend.

Heat olive oil in a large nonstick skillet or Dutch oven over medium-high heat. Add pork and cook 2 to 3 minutes, stirring occasionally, until browned.

Stir in salsa, preserves, and pineapple. Reduce heat to medium and cook, uncovered, 10 minutes, stirring once. Serve over rice.

Yield: 4 servings.

Note: 1 (1.25-ounce) package taco seasoning mix may be substituted for Mexican blend.

Per serving: 635 calories, 9.6 g. fat, 18 mg. cholesterol, 969 mg. sodium

How did we get the name for this dish? When you read the ingredients for this recipe, they sound as if several cuisines—from Southwestern to Caribbean—were jumbled together. Thus, the name "Mumba Jumba." Ask your family what they would name this dish.

Marco Polo Chicken

This dish was inspired by Country Captain, a chicken recipe popular in Colonial times. Our version omits the step of deep-frying the chicken and adds spices such as curry powder. That's why we call it Marco Polo chicken—the dish still has the spirit of exploration found in County Captain, but now it's even better.

2-2½ pounds chicken thighs
1 teaspoon garlic powder
1 teaspoon salt
1 teaspoon pepper
1 tablespoon olive oil
1 (10-ounce) package frozen onion, celery, and pepper
3 cloves garlic, minced
1 (28-ounce) can diced tomatoes, undrained
⅓ cup raisins
1 tablespoon brown sugar
2 teaspoons curry powder
½ teaspoon dried thyme
1 cup couscous, uncooked
1½ cups water
½ teaspoon salt
⅓ cup slivered almonds (optional)

Remove large pieces of skin from tops of thighs; discard skin. Sprinkle both sides of chicken with garlic powder, salt, and pepper.

Heat oil in a large Dutch oven over medium-high heat. Add chicken and cook 5 minutes on each side until lightly browned. (You may have to brown chicken in batches if overcrowded to avoid steaming chicken.) Remove chicken; set aside.

Chicken thighs go easy on the budget, and, because the meat is dark, offer plenty of iron. They also boast a slightly higher fat content than white meat—and thus, more flavor. If you don't want to serve whole thighs, simply remove, pull meat from bones, and chop them after they cook. Add meat back to the pot before serving. You may also substitute four boneless breasts. The breasts will cook slightly faster than the thighs.

Add frozen onion blend and garlic to Dutch oven. Cook 3 minutes until tender.

Add tomatoes, raisins, brown sugar, curry, and thyme. Return chicken to tomato mixture; stir well. Bring to a boil; decrease heat to low; simmer, uncovered, 20 minutes or until chicken is done.

While chicken simmers, boil 1½ cups water in a medium saucepan. Add couscous and ½ teaspoon salt. Remove from heat, cover, and let stand 5 to 7 minutes. Fluff with a fork before serving.

To serve, spoon chicken mixture over couscous, and sprinkle with almonds, if desired.

Yield: 4 servings.

Note: 1 onion, chopped and 1 green bell pepper, chopped may be substituted for frozen onion mixture.

■ ■ ■ ■ ■ ■ ■ ■ ■

If you haven't tried couscous, you're in for a treat. It cooks faster than rice, and it offers a slightly nutty flavor. Look for it in the rice/ grains section of the supermarket.

■ ■ ■ ■ ■ ■ ■ ■ ■

30-Minute Red Beans and Rice

1 (6.2-ounce) package long grain and wild rice

1 tablespoon olive or vegetable oil

1 pound smoked link turkey sausage, cut into ½-inch slices

1 (10-ounce) package frozen onion, celery, and pepper

2 (15-ounce) cans kidney beans, undrained

1 (14.5-ounce) can diced tomatoes with roasted garlic, undrained

½ teaspoon Cajun Seasoning Blend (page 178)

Hot sauce (optional)

Cook rice according to package directions without seasoning packet, omitting butter. Cover and keep warm.

Meanwhile, heat oil in a large nonstick skillet over medium heat. Add sausage and frozen onion, and cook 3 minutes, stirring occasionally, until tender.

Add beans, tomatoes, and Cajun Seasoning Blend; cook 5 minutes. Reduce heat to medium-low, and cook 5 minutes. Serve over rice with hot sauce, if desired.

Yield: 4 servings.

Note: ½ teaspoon dried thyme and ¼ teaspoon pepper may be substituted for Cajun blend.

Creamy Italian Rice Skillet

1 tablespoon olive oil
2 cloves garlic, chopped
1 cup Arborio rice, uncooked
2 (16-ounce) cans vegetable or chicken broth
1 (9-ounce) package frozen chopped spinach, thawed
10 sun-dried tomato halves, cut into pieces
½ cup shredded fontina or Swiss cheese
¼ cup freshly grated Parmesan cheese
½ teaspoon freshly ground pepper

Heat oil in a large saucepan over medium heat; add garlic and cook 2 minutes.

Add rice, stirring until coated. Stir in broth, spinach, and tomatoes.

Bring mixture to a boil, reduce heat, and simmer, stirring often over medium heat 20 to 25 minutes or until liquid evaporates and rice is tender. Stir in cheeses and pepper.

Yield: 4 main dish servings or 6 side dish servings.

Arborio rice (found in large supermarkets or specialty stores) has short, fat kernels that yield a creamy texture in dishes similar to this risotto.

Wow, Mama! Black Beans and Rice

1 clove garlic, minced
1 (10-ounce) package frozen onion, celery, and pepper
1 (15.5-ounce) can black beans, undrained
1 (10-ounce) can mild enchilada sauce
Hot cooked long-grain or brown rice
Chopped fresh tomatoes
Shredded Cheddar Cheese
Reduced-fat sour cream

Coat a medium nonstick skillet with cooking spray. Place skillet over medium-high heat. Add garlic and frozen onion. Cook 3 to 5 minutes, stirring occasionally.

Add beans and enchilada sauce. Cook 5 minutes, stirring occasionally, or until beans are heated through and mixture is slightly thick.

To serve, spoon beans over rice and top with tomatoes, cheese, and sour cream.

Yield: 4 servings.

Black Beans and Rice with Sausage:
One pound ground Italian sausage or 1 pound ground turkey sausage may be cooked, drained, and added to black bean mixture at the end of cooking. Simmer gently until heated through.

Note: 1 onion, chopped and 1 green bell pepper may be substituted for frozen blend. Believe it or not, the black beans are excellent spooned over Cheese Grits (page 132). Try this combo when you're feeding a crowd that prefers meatless dishes—or if you just want something different.

Simple Seafood Paella

1 tablespoon olive oil
1 pound kielbasa sausage, sliced
1 onion, chopped
2 cloves garlic, minced
1 (10-ounce) package saffron-flavored
  yellow rice mix
3 cups reduced-sodium chicken broth or
  water
2 (14.5-ounce) cans pasta-style tomatoes
1 (14-ounce) can quartered artichoke
  hearts, rinsed and drained
1 (10-ounce) package frozen English
  peas
1 pound medium-size fresh shrimp,
  peeled and deveined

Heat olive oil in a Dutch oven or large, heavy saucepan over medium-high heat; add sausage, onion, and garlic. Cook 3 to 5 minutes, stirring constantly; drain, if desired.

Add rice, broth, tomatoes, and artichoke hearts; bring to a boil. Cover, reduce heat and simmer 10 minutes.

Stir in peas and shrimp. Cover and cook 5 minutes or until shrimp are pink and tender. Remove lid and stir well. If needed, cook until liquid is absorbed.

Yield: 6 servings.

Chicken and Sausage Paella:
Cook 4 boneless chicken breasts, cut into strips, in 2 tablespoons olive oil with onion and garlic. Proceed with recipe, omitting shrimp.

■ ■ ■ ■ ■ ■ ■ ■ ■
Paella is a Spanish rice dish flavored with saffron. It is typically prepared in a round, shallow paella pan, but our version simmers on the cooktop in less than half the time.

Summer Squash Skillet

Classified as summer squashes, zucchini and yellow squash have soft, edible skin and seeds. Winter squash, such as pumpkins and acorns, have tough skin and seeds that are removed before serving.

2 tablespoons butter or olive oil
2 cloves garlic, minced
1 onion, quartered and sliced
2 zucchini squash, sliced
2 yellow squash, sliced
2 tomatoes, chopped
1 tablespoon chopped fresh basil
1 teaspoon chopped fresh thyme
½ teaspoon salt
⅓ cup freshly grated Parmesan cheese

Melt butter in a large skillet; add garlic and onion and cook 3 minutes over medium heat until tender. Add squash and cook 5 to 8 minutes, stirring often, until tender.

Stir in tomato, basil, thyme, and salt. Cook 3 minutes or until hot. Sprinkle with Parmesan cheese.

Yield: 4 main dish servings or 8 side dish servings.

Note: ½ teaspoon dried Italian herbs may be substituted for the fresh basil and thyme

Per serving: 165 calories, 10.4 g. fat, 29 mg. cholesterol, 498 mg. sodium

Vegetable Stir Fry

This recipe cooks fast so you'll want everything mixed, chopped, and measured before you begin.

¾ cup vegetable or fat-free chicken broth
¼ cup reduced-sodium soy sauce
2 tablespoons lime juice
1 tablespoon cornstarch
1 tablespoon creamy peanut butter
1 tablespoon chili paste with garlic (optional)
1 tablespoon canola or vegetable oil
2 cloves garlic, minced
1 onion, quartered and sliced
1 red bell pepper, thinly sliced
2 zucchini, halved and sliced
2 yellow squash, halved and sliced
1 (8-ounce) package mushrooms, sliced
2 tablespoons chopped fresh cilantro
4 cups hot cooked rice

Combine broth, soy sauce, juice, cornstarch, peanut butter, and chili paste in a small bowl; set aside.

Heat oil in a wok or very large skillet over medium-high heat. Add garlic, onion, and bell pepper; cook 3 minutes, stirring constantly, until slightly tender.

Add zucchini, squash, and mushrooms; cook, stirring constantly 5 minutes or until crisp-tender.

Stir in broth mixture; bring to a boil. Boil 1 minute until thickened; stir in cilantro. Serve over hot cooked rice.

Yield: 4 servings.

Per serving: 379 calories, 6.6 g. fat, 0 mg. cholesterol, 729 mg. sodium

Stir-fries are great ways to use leftovers and pieces of fresh vegetables. The chopping part is always longer than the cooking part. For speedier prep, raid the salad bar at your supermarket for pre-cut vegetables.

Fall Pork Chop Skillet

½ teaspoon ground allspice

½ teaspoon ground ginger

¼ teaspoon salt

¼ teaspoon pepper

4 (1-inch thick) center cut boneless pork chops

1 (15-ounce) can unsweetened chunk pineapple, undrained

2 tablespoons light brown sugar

½ cup orange juice

2 teaspoons soy sauce

2 small sweet potato, peeled and cut lengthwise into 4 slices

1 small acorn squash, cut into 4 rings

1 cooking apple, cored and cut into 4 slices

Combine allspice, ginger, salt, and pepper; rub over pork chops and set aside. Drain pineapple, reserving liquid. Combine pineapple liquid, brown sugar, orange juice, and soy sauce; set aside.

Coat a large nonstick skillet with vegetable cooking spray; place over medium-high heat until hot. Add chops and cook 3 minutes on each side until brown.

Layer sweet potato, squash, and pineapple chunks over pork chops. Pour juice mixture over chops. Cover, reduce heat to low, and simmer 15 minutes. Add apple slices; cover and cook an additional 5 minutes.

Yield: 4 servings.

Per serving: 507 calories, 19.5 g. fat, 94 mg. cholesterol, 396 mg. sodium

Creamy Pecan Chicken

1 tablespoon butter
½ cup chopped pecans
¼ teaspoon garlic powder
6 boneless chicken breasts
1½ cups heavy whipping cream
3 tablespoons peach preserves
1 tablespoon Dijon mustard
¼ teaspoon salt
¼ teaspoon pepper
¼ teaspoon cayenne pepper, optional
Hot cooked fettuccine or rice

Melt butter in a large nonstick skillet over medium-high heat. Add pecans and garlic powder; cook 2 minutes until very lightly toasted (you'll smell a nice pecan aroma). Remove from skillet and set aside.

Cook chicken in skillet 2 minutes on each side or until lightly browned. Reduce heat to medium. Add cream, preserves, mustard, salt, pepper, and half of pecan mixture, stirring well.

Cook, uncovered, 10 to 12 minutes or until sauce thickens slightly and chicken is tender. Serve over pasta or rice and sprinkle with remaining pecans.

Yield: 6 servings.

This is a rich, elegant recipe—great for company or special family meals. In spring, serve with steamed asparagus; in fall or winter, try steamed broccoli.

Brown-Buttered Trout with Almonds

This recipe cooks fast and is best served hot, so have your side dishes ready and the table set!

½ cup all-purpose flour
½ teaspoon pepper
4 boneless trout fillet, skin removed (if desired)
½ cup butter, divided
⅓ cup sliced almonds
2 tablespoons fresh lemon juice
1 teaspoon Worcestershire sauce
2 tablespoons chopped fresh parsley

Combine flour and pepper in a shallow bowl; dredge trout in flour mixture and set aside.

Melt 2 tablespoons butter in a large skillet over medium heat. Cook fillets 4 to 6 minutes, turning once, until tender and golden (add additional tablespoon butter if necessary). Place trout on serving platter and keep warm.

Add remaining butter and nuts to skillet; cook over medium heat 1 to 3 minutes until lightly browned. Add lemon juice and Worcestershire sauce. Remove from heat and stir in parsley; pour over fillets, and serve immediately.

Yield: 4 servings.

Fresh catfish or tilapia fillets may be substituted for the trout.

Pecan-Buttered Catfish:
Substitute fresh catfish for the trout and chopped pecans for the almonds. Use ½ to 1 teaspoon Mrs. Dash in place of pepper.

Casseroles

One cannot think well, love well,
sleep well, if one has not
dined well.

Virginia Woolf

Conversation Starters

- ## WHICH FORK?
If the kids break a sweat when confronted with an elaborate meal, gradually build up to the formal dinner. For the first week, emphasize asking to be excused from the table at the end of the meal. The next week, work on simple etiquette such as not talking with your mouth full. Later point out which is the salad fork, etc. After about four weeks, plan a formal meal where everyone practices their dining skills.

Need some help with those place settings? Go to the library and ask for book recommendations on etiquette and dining skills for children.

- ## PRECIOUS PLATES
The Red Plate Company markets bright red dinner plates for special occasions. Available at specialty stores and gift shops, the plates come with a permanent marker to use on the back of the dish. Families note the honorees, dates, and occasions of use. Whoever is celebrating a birthday, good report card, promotion, etc., uses the red plate on his or her special night. If you'd like to create your own plate, check out a ceramics studio. Permanent markers may be purchased wherever office or art supplies are sold.

Italian Penne Pasta Casserole

16 ounces penne pasta
1 pound extra lean ground beef
1 (10-ounce) package frozen onion, celery and pepper
1 (8-ounce) package sliced mushrooms
2 (14.5-ounce) stewed Italian-style tomatoes
1 (10¾-ounce) can Cheddar cheese soup
½ cup Parmesan cheese
½ cup dry breadcrumbs

Preheat oven to 350°.

Cook pasta according to package directions, omitting salt and fat; drain.

Brown ground beef in a large nonstick skillet or Dutch oven over medium-high heat, 3 to 5 minutes (or until meat is no longer pink), crumbling with a wooden spoon; drain. Add frozen onion and mushrooms. Cook until tender, about 3 minutes. Add stewed tomatoes.

Pour cooked pasta into lightly greased 13 x 9-inch casserole. Pour cheese soup over pasta and toss to coat. Pour tomato-meat mixture over cheese-coated penne. Sprinkle with Parmesan cheese and breadcrumbs.

Bake 35 to 40 minutes or until edges of pasta start to brown. To make ahead, layer the casserole and refrigerate; bake 45 to 50 minutes, and serve hot out of the oven.

Yield: 8 servings.

Note: If you can't find Italian-style stewed tomatoes, simply substitute 2 (14.5-ounce) cans plain stewed tomatoes and 1 teaspoon Italian seasoning. You can also substitute 1 onion, chopped and 1 green pepper, chopped for the frozen onion mixture.

Per serving: 454 calories, 14.6 g. fat, 48 mg. cholesterol, 598 mg. sodium

Add a tossed salad and garlic bread for a classic Italian repast. Wine? We like Chianti.

kid friendly

Speedy Microwave Lasagna

This time-saving recipe eliminates boiling the noodles and trims almost 30 minutes off the cooking time for lasagna. Toss a green salad with fresh orange or grapefruit slices and balsamic vinaigrette while the casserole cooks.

1½ pounds ground chuck
1 (28-ounce) jar spaghetti sauce
¾ cup red wine or water
2 cups low-fat cottage cheese
2 large eggs
1 teaspoon dried whole thyme
8 lasagna noodles, uncooked
2 cups shredded mozzarella cheese
½ cup grated Parmesan cheese

Crumble beef in a large bowl. Microwave at HIGH 4 minutes; stir and microwave 2 more minutes or meat is no longer pink, stirring once; drain. Stir in spaghetti sauce and wine.

Stir together cottage cheese, eggs, and thyme.

Spread 1 cup meat sauce in a lightly greased 13- x 9-inch baking dish. Layer ingredients in dish in this order: 4 noodles, half of meat sauce, half of cottage cheese mixture, half of mozzarella cheese, 4 noodles, remaining meat sauce, cottage cheese, and mozzarella cheese. Cover with heavy-duty plastic wrap. Unfold one corner of wrap to allow steam to escape.

Microwave at HIGH 8 minutes. Microwave at MEDIUM (50% power) 30 minutes or until noodles are tender when tested with a fork, turning dish twice during cooking.

Sprinkle with Parmesan cheese; let stand 10 minutes before serving.

Yield: 6 to 8 servings.

Beefy Tex-Mex Casserole

1 pound lean ground beef
2 (14.5-ounce) cans Mexican-style stewed tomatoes, undrained
1 (16-ounce) can chili hot beans, undrained
1 (2.25-ounce) can sliced ripe olives, drained
½ teaspoon chili powder
1 teaspoon garlic powder
3 cups corn chips, lightly crushed
½ cup loosely packed fresh cilantro
2 cups (8 ounces) shredded Monterey Jack cheese

Preheat oven to 350°.

Brown ground beef in a large nonstick skillet over medium-high heat, 3 to 5 minutes (or until no longer pink), crumbling with a wooden spoon; drain.

Add tomatoes, chili beans, olives, chili powder, and garlic powder, stirring well. Cook 5 minutes.

Place half of crushed corn chips in bottom of lightly greased 13- x 9-inch baking dish. Spoon half of beef mixture over chips. Repeat with remaining chips and beef. Sprinkle with fresh cilantro and cheese.

Bake 30 minutes or until bubbly and heated through.

Yield: 6 servings.

Beefy Polenta Casserole:
Follow directions substituting 1 (16-ounce) package refrigerated polenta for the corn chips. Cut polenta into ½-inch-thick slices. Place polenta slices on bottom of casserole, and top with ground beef mixture, cilantro, and cheese. Bake as directed.

The signature ingredients of Tex-Mex—beef, beans, tomatoes—two-step their way to a quick and easy meal. Serve with guacamole and chips and a green salad.

Don't worry about chopping cilantro. We just plucked the whole leaves off the stems and threw them in the measuring cup. If you have a compulsive attack and have to chop, use less. Chopping the herb intensifies the flavor.

Stuffed Peppers with Golden Rice

Boost the flavor of a traditional stuffed pepper with this Middle Eastern twist featuring saffron rice, raisins, and almonds. If you have leftover meat loaf, use it in place of the ground meat. The baked peppers also freeze nicely.

- 1 (5-ounce) package yellow rice with seasonings
- 6 large green or red bell peppers
- 1 tablespoon olive oil
- 1 clove garlic, minced
- 1 (10-ounce) package frozen onion, celery, and pepper
- ½ pound extra lean ground beef or turkey
- ½ cup slivered almonds
- ¼ cup raisins (optional)
- 1 (28-ounce) jar spaghetti sauce

Preheat oven to 350°.

Cook rice mix according to package directions; set aside.

Meanwhile, cut off 1-inch of the top of each pepper and remove the seeds. Place peppers in a lightly greased 11- x 7-inch baking dish.

Heat 1 tablespoon olive oil in a nonstick skillet over medium-high heat. Add garlic and frozen onion. Cook, stirring occasionally, 3 to 5 minutes or until liquid has evaporated.

Add ground meat to skillet; brown 3 to 5 minutes (or until no longer pink), crumbling with a wooden spoon. Stir in almonds, cooked yellow rice, and, if desired, raisins. Add ½ cup spaghetti sauce, and cook until thoroughly heated.

Bell peppers are available in a variety of colors: red, green, white, purple, brown, yellow, and orange. Red bells are simply green bell peppers that have been allowed to ripen (and sweeten, too).

Spoon hot meat mixture into the peppers, pressing meat down into peppers with a spoon. Spoon 1 tablespoon spaghetti sauce over each pepper. Pour remaining sauce into bottom of the baking dish, around peppers.

Bake 30 to 45 minutes or until peppers are soft and the filling is hot.

Yield: 6 servings.

Note: Substitute 1 onion, chopped and 1 green pepper, chopped for frozen onion mixture.

Per serving: 430 calories, 20.4 g. fat, 26 mg. cholesterol, 692 mg. sodium

Crispy Chicken 'n' Rice Casserole

1 tablespoon olive oil
1 (8-ounce) package sliced fresh mushrooms
1 (8-ounce) can sliced water chestnuts, drained
1 small onion, chopped
3 stalks celery, sliced
1 cup cooked rice
2 cups chopped cooked chicken
1 (10¾-ounce) can reduced-fat cream of mushroom soup
¾ cup light mayonnaise
1 tablespoon fresh lemon juice
⅓ cup slivered almonds
1 cup crushed corn flakes

Preheat oven to 350°.

Place oil in a large nonstick skillet over medium-high heat. Add mushrooms, water chestnuts, onion, and celery. Cook, stirring occasionally, 3 to 5 minutes; remove from heat. Drain, if necessary.

Combine rice, chicken, soup, mayonnaise, lemon juice, and almonds in a large bowl. Stir in cooked vegetables. Pour into lightly greased 13- x 9-inch baking dish. Sprinkle with crushed corn flakes. Bake 30 minutes or until bubbly and heated through.

Yield: 10 servings.

Note: Other topping options include 1 cup crushed potato chips or 2 cups fat-free salad croutons.

Per serving: 243 calories, 11.1 g. fat, 31 mg. cholesterol, 466 mg. sodium

Quick Curried Chicken Divan

No time to cook chicken? Use a roasted chicken from the deli. This is also a good make-ahead recipe.

2 (10-ounce) packages frozen broccoli florets, thawed and drained

2 cups diced cooked chicken or turkey

1 (8-ounce) package sharp shredded Cheddar cheese, divided

1 (10¾-ounce) can reduced-fat cream of roasted garlic soup or cream of mushroom soup

½ cup skim milk

1 cup reduced-fat mayonnaise

⅓ cup Parmesan cheese

1 teaspoon curry powder

½ teaspoon garlic powder

Paprika

Preheat oven to 350°.

Arrange broccoli in a lightly greased 11- x 7- inch baking dish. Top with chicken. Sprinkle half of cheese over chicken.

Combine soup, milk, mayonnaise, Parmesan cheese, curry powder, and garlic powder; pour mixture over cheese.

Bake for 25 minutes. Sprinkle with remaining Cheddar cheese and paprika. Bake an additional 5 minutes.

Yield: 6 servings.

Note: You may thaw broccoli in a bowl in your microwave. Set microwave on DEFROST, and cook 10 to 12 minutes. Drain well, or the casserole will be watery.

Curry powder is actually a blend of ground herbs, spices, and seeds. Turmeric gives curry dishes the bright yellow color. Fresh curry is used extensively in Indian cooking. The red and green curries of Thai cuisine taste dramatically different from commercial curry powder.

Chicken Enchilada Bake

Tortillas are easier to work with if you microwave them (wrapped in a damp paper towel) 60 seconds at HIGH.

1 cup commercial tomatillo sauce or salsa
1 (11-ounce) can corn kernels, drained
1 (2¼-ounce) can ripe olives, drained
¼ cup chopped fresh cilantro
8 (6-inch) corn tortillas
2 cups chopped cooked chicken
1¼ cups low-fat cottage cheese
1 (10-ounce) can enchilada sauce
1½-2 cups shredded Cheddar cheese

Preheat oven to 350°.

Stir together 1 cup tomatillo sauce, corn, olives, and cilantro; set aside.

Place tortillas on flat surface, and spoon ¼ cup chicken and 2 tablespoons cottage cheese down center of each. Roll up and place seam-side-down in lightly greased 13- x 9-inch baking dish.

Pour enchilada sauce over rolled tortillas. Spoon corn mixture down center of tortillas and around sides; sprinkle with cheese.

Bake 30 minutes. Let stand 5 minutes before serving.

Yield: 4 to 6 servings.

Note: 1½ cups light sour cream and larger flour tortillas may be substituted for cottage cheese and corn tortillas.

Shrimp-and-Artichoke Casserole

Many supermarkets will steam shrimp for you at no extra cost.

½ cup butter
1 onion, chopped
3 green onions, sliced
1 (8-ounce) package sliced fresh mushrooms
½ cup all-purpose flour
1 cup dry white wine
2 cups half-and-half
1 teaspoon salt
¼ teaspoon cayenne or ground red pepper
2 tablespoons chopped fresh parsley
1 cup shredded Swiss cheese
2 (14-ounce) cans quartered artichoke hearts, rinsed and drained
1 pound shrimp, boiled or steamed and peeled and deveined
¼ cup grated Romano or Parmesan cheese

Preheat oven to 350°.

Melt butter in a large skillet over medium-high heat. Add onions and mushrooms; cook 3 minutes, stirring occasionally, or until tender. Stir in flour; cook 1 minute.

Stir in wine, half-and-half, salt, and pepper; cook, stirring constantly, 3 to 5 minutes or until thick and bubbly. Stir in parsley and Swiss cheese.

Combine artichoke hearts and shrimp in a lightly greased 13- x 9-inch baking dish. Pour sauce over shrimp and sprinkle with cheese.

Bake 30 to 40 minutes until golden brown. Serve as a casserole or over hot cooked rice, fettuccine, or toasted French baguette halves.

Yield: 6 to 8 servings.

Shrimp are considered a crustacean (shellfish) and come in many colors and sizes. Can you guess how many legs a shrimp has? Most have 10.

Company Lasagna Alfredo

Try this when you entertain after work. Using a deli-roasted chicken and commercial Alfredo sauce saves time. The dish may also be made ahead, refrigerated, and reheated in the microwave.

9 lasagna noodles
1 teaspoon olive oil
2 stalks celery
2 cloves garlic, minced
1 onion, chopped
4 cups coarsely chopped, cooked chicken
2 (10-ounce) packages light Alfredo sauce
1 teaspoon fresh or dried rosemary
1 (12-ounce) jar roasted red peppers
   (no oil added), drained
¼ cup grated Parmesan cheese
¼ teaspoon black pepper
⅓ cup slivered almonds

Preheat oven to 350°.

Cook lasagna noodles according to package directions; drain. To keep them from sticking together, spray wax paper with vegetable cooking spray, and layer noodles between sheets of wax paper until ready for use.

Place oil in a nonstick skillet over medium heat. Add celery, garlic, and onion. Cook, stirring occasionally, 3 minutes or until vegetables are crisp-tender. Remove from heat, and set aside.

Combine chicken, onion-celery mixture, Alfredo sauce, and rosemary in a large bowl. Layer ingredients in a lightly greased 11- x 7-inch baking dish in this order: 3 noodles, one-third of chicken mixture, roasted red peppers, 3 noodles, half of remaining chicken mixture, 3 noodles, remaining chicken mixture.

Top casserole with Parmesan cheese, pepper, and almonds. Bake for 40 minutes until heated through. Remove from oven, and let stand 10 minutes before serving.

Yield: 8 servings.

Note: one (3-pound) rotisserie chicken yields 4 cups chopped cooked chicken

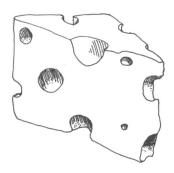

Rotisserie chicken—also known as deli-roasted chicken—is available in many large supermarkets. You can also find precooked whole chickens in the meat case. Any of these options work well when you need chopped, cooked chicken quick.

Captain's Tuna Hot Dish

Older kids may be able to make this without assistance. Tiny tots enjoy sprinkling the goldfish crackers on top.

In the Midwest, what we southerners know as a casserole sometimes goes by the name "hot dish." Anywhere you live, however, you'll love this classic.

8 ounces small sea shell pasta

1 (10-ounce) package frozen onion, celery, and pepper

2 (6-ounce) cans tuna packed in water, drained

1 (10¾-ounce) can reduced-fat cream of mushroom soup with roasted garlic and herbs

1 cup light sour cream

½ teaspoon salt

½ teaspoon pepper

¼ cup fresh chopped parsley (optional)

Topping options: fish-shaped crackers; or crunchy topping for broccoli casserole (page 137); or reduced-fat cheese crackers, crushed

Preheat oven to 350°.

Cook pasta according to package directions, omitting salt and fat; drain.

Meanwhile, coat nonstick skillet with cooking spray, and place over medium heat; add frozen onion, and cook 3 to 5 minutes, stirring occasionally, or until onions are tender and moisture is gone. Remove from heat.

Add tuna, mushroom soup, sour cream, salt, pepper, and, if desired, parsley.

Stir tuna mixture into cooked pasta, mixing well.

Pour into a lightly greased 11- x 7-inch baking dish. Sprinkle with your choice of topping. Bake for 25 minutes or until bubbly and heated through.

Yield: 6 servings.

Note: Substitute 1 onion, chopped and 1 green pepper, chopped for frozen onion mixture.

From the Oven

No mean woman can cook well,
for it calls for a light head, a
generous spirit and a large heart.

Paul Gaugin

Conversation Starters

- **COSTUME PARTY**

Any day of the year, you can invite your ghouls and goblins to come to the table dressed for Halloween.

- **HOME SWEET HOME**

These questions about your home will get your family talking.

1. What's the best room in the house?
2. The most fun?
3. The quietest?
4. The scariest?
5. The brightest?
6. The darkest?
7 The most unique?

Italian Broiled Steak

1 (1¼- to 1½-pound) boneless beef top
    sirloin steak or flank steak
2 tablespoon lite soy sauce
1 tablespoon dried Italian seasoning
1 teaspoon garlic powder

Trim any visible fat from steak. Brush soy
sauce evenly on both sides of steak. Sprinkle
evenly with Italian seasoning and garlic
powder.

Broil steak 3 inches from heat (with electric
oven door partially open) 6 to 8 minutes on
each side, or until meat is cooked to desired
doneness.

Slice steak diagonally across grain into thin
slices.

Yield: 4 servings.

Note: See page 146 for a tasty beef salad idea.

■ ■ ■ ■ ■ ■ ■ ■ ■

**Broiling gives the
same crispy outer
coating that grilling
does. Using a rub
eliminates the
standing time
needed for a mari-
nade.**

Mucho Bueno Meat Loaf

Mucho Bueno means "very good" in Spanish. Ask each member of your family what his or her favorite food is, and guess the country of origin.

The vegetable soup mix and salsa add healthy ingredients as well as flavor to this quick and easy meat loaf. Serve it with mashed potatoes and steamed green beans.

1 pound ground chuck (or lean ground beef)
¾ cup quick-cooking oats
1 (1.4-ounce) package vegetable soup mix
½ cup commercial chunky salsa
1 large egg

Preheat oven to 350°.

Combine all ingredients. Using your hands, shape meat into a 7- x 2-inch loaf.

Line the base of a roasting pan with foil. Coat the foil with vegetable cooking spray. Cover the pan with the rack. Coat rack with vegetable cooking spray. Place meat on the rack, and bake for 45 to 50 minutes or until done. (To test for doneness, gently cut into the loaf with a fork. You shouldn't see any pink.)

Yield: 4 to 6 servings.

New-Fashioned Salmon Patties

1 (7½-ounce) can pink salmon, drained
10 saltine crackers, crushed (about
    ½ cup)
¼ cup yellow cornmeal
2 large eggs, lightly beaten
½ teaspoon dried dill weed
¼ teaspoon onion powder
¼ teaspoon pepper
1-3 tablespoons milk
Creamy Dill Sauce

Preheat oven to 400°.

Stir together salmon, cracker crumbs, cornmeal, eggs, dill weed, onion powder, and pepper. Add milk, 1 tablespoon at a time, as needed. (These patties do best if this mixture is very wet.) With your hands, shape into 4 patties.

Place on a baking sheet coated with vegetable cooking spray. Bake 20 minutes; do not turn. Serve with Creamy Dill Sauce.

Yield: 4 servings

Creamy Dill Sauce:
⅓ cup mayonnaise
2 tablespoons Dijon mustard
2 tablespoons dill cubes or chopped dill
    pickles

Combine all ingredients.

Yield: ½ cup.

Pan-Fried Salmon Patties:
Follow directions to mix patties. Place 1 tablespoon oil in a nonstick skillet over medium-high heat; add patties. Let brown on one side, about 2 minutes. Turn; reduce heat to medium, and cook 5 additional minutes. Serve with Creamy Dill Sauce.

Adding a dilly of a sauce updates the traditional salmon patty from Susan's mom.

Sesame-Crusted Salmon

This salmon is good—but the crust makes it great!

1 (2-pound) fresh salmon fillet, skinned and cut into 4 pieces
1 tablespoon soy sauce
1 teaspoon sesame oil
1 cup crushed regular potato chips
1 tablespoon sesame seeds
Lime-Ginger Butter

Preheat oven to 375°.

Brush salmon filets with soy sauce and sesame oil.

Combine crushed chips and sesame seeds. Roll salmon into chip mixture and place on a lightly greased foil-lined baking sheet.

Bake for 15 minutes or until fish flakes easily with a fork. Serve with Lime-Ginger Butter.

Yield: 4 servings.

Lime-Ginger Butter:
4 tablespoons butter
1 teaspoon grated lime rind
¼ teaspoon grated ginger

Combine ingredients. Chill until serving.

Yield: ¼ cup.

Sesame seeds are reportedly the first recorded seasoning used. For more than 5,000 years, sesame seeds have been used for breads, garnishes, oils, and desserts.

Oven BBQ Shrimp

They're a mess to shell, but oh-so-good to eat.

½ cup butter
½ cup beer
2 lemons, sliced
2 cloves garlic, pressed
½ teaspoon freshly ground pepper
1 teaspoon Italian seasoning
1 tablespoons Worcestershire sauce
1 tablespoons hot pepper sauce
1½ pounds unpeeled, medium-size fresh
   shrimp, shell-on
Hot French bread

Preheat oven to 400°.

Melt butter in a large roasting pan. Stir in beer, lemon slices, garlic, pepper, Italian seasoning, Worcestershire, pepper sauce, and shrimp.

Bake for 15 minutes, stirring occasionally, until shrimp are done. Serve with hot French bread for sopping up liquid.

Yield: 4 servings.

For easy clean-up, serve the shrimp on newspapers with plenty of paper towels.

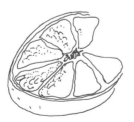

Apricot-Stuffed Pork Loin Chops

Simple enough for every day but impressive enough for special occasions, this recipe, from Julia, is one of our favorites.

10 dried apricot halves
¼ cup chopped pecans
1 clove garlic
2 tablespoons molasses, divided
2 teaspoons chopped fresh thyme
¼ teaspoon salt
¼ teaspoon pepper
4 (1-inch thick) boneless pork chops
¾ cup chicken broth
½ cup whipping cream
2 teaspoons all-purpose flour

Preheat oven to 350°.

Combine apricots, pecans, garlic, 1 tablespoon molasses, thyme, salt, and pepper in container of food processor. Pulse 5 or 6 times until finely chopped. (Mixture may be finely chopped by hand, if desired.)

Trim excess fat from each pork chop and cut slit in side to make pocket. Stuff evenly with apricot mixture. Pinch edges closed and secure with toothpick, if necessary.

Brush chops with remaining 1 tablespoon molasses. Place in lightly greased baking or roasting pan, and bake 25 minutes or until done, and a meat thermometer registers 160°. (Chops should be slightly pink inside.)

Remove toothpick, and place chops on serving platter; keep warm. Place pan on cooktop over medium-high heat. Add chicken broth, and stir occasionally to loosen cooked bits.

Combine whipping cream and flour, blending well. Stir into broth, and cook 3 minutes or until slightly thickened. Serve sauce over chops.

Yield: 4 servings.

Note: 1 teaspoon dried thyme may be substituted for fresh.

Oven-Fried Chicken Fingers

½ cup sour cream

2 tablespoons milk

4 boneless, skinless chicken breast halves, cut into ¼-inch slices

½ cup seasoned dry breadcrumbs

½ cup cracker crumbs (about 10 saltine crackers)

¼ cup all-purpose flour

1 teaspoon paprika

½ teaspoon salt

½ teaspoon garlic powder

Honey-Mustard Sauce

Preheat oven to 400°.

Combine sour cream and milk. (Mixture will be thick). Dredge chicken strips in sour cream mixture, shaking excess.

Combine breadcrumbs, cracker crumbs, flour, paprika, salt, and garlic powder. Coat chicken in breadcrumb mixture and place on a lightly greased baking sheet.

Bake for 14 minutes or until golden brown, turning once. Serve with Honey-Mustard Sauce.

Yield: 4 to 6 servings.

Honey-Mustard Sauce:

Any extra sauce makes a tangy spread for ham or turkey sandwiches.

⅓ cup Dijon mustard

3 tablespoons honey

Combine ingredients.

Yield: ⅓ cup.

Per serving: 331 calories, 8.8 g. fat, 65 mg. cholesterol, 855 mg. sodium

Roasted Chicken with Rosemary Gravy

1 large lemon
2 tablespoons olive oil
¼ teaspoon salt
½ teaspoon pepper
2 teaspoons chopped fresh rosemary
1 (4½-pound) whole chicken
½ cup chicken broth
1 tablespoon all-purpose flour

Preheat oven to 400°.

Halve lemon and juice into small bowl, reserving lemon halves. Add olive oil, salt, pepper, and rosemary.

Remove neck and giblets from chicken; rinse chicken and place lemon halves in body cavity. Pull skin gently away from meat to form pockets. Spoon all but 1 teaspoon juice mixture under skin. Rub remaining 1 teaspoon juice mixture over skin. Place chicken in a large roasting pan. (If skin is torn; use wooden picks to secure it over breast meat to prevent overcooking breast meat.)

Bake 1 hour to 1 hour and 15 minutes or until done. (Juices will run clear when chicken is pierced with knife.) Place chicken on serving platter; keep warm.

Skim any fat from roasting pan and discard.

Combine broth and flour. Stir broth mixture into pan drippings. Cook over medium-high heat 1 to 2 minutes or until thickened, scraping bits from bottom of pan. Serve gravy with roasted chicken.

Yield: 4 servings.

Two good reasons to roast chicken tonight: It is inexpensive to make and it smells heavenly.

Grilled-Chicken Pot Pie

kid friendly

You can substitute any frozen vegetable for the green beans and carrots; just use an equal amount.

4 tablespoons butter
3 stalks celery, chopped
½ medium onion, chopped
¼ cup all-purpose flour
1 cup chicken broth
1 cup half-and-half
3 cups chopped grilled chicken
1 cup frozen baby green beans and carrots, thawed and cut into pieces
1-2 teaspoons herb chicken seasoning or poultry seasoning
1 (15-ounce) package refrigerated pie crusts
1 egg
1 tablespoon water

Preheat oven to 375°.

Melt butter in a large saucepan. Cook celery and onion 5 minutes until tender.

Stir in flour; cook 1 minute.

Add broth and half-and-half, stirring until well blended. Cook 5 minutes or until thickened and bubbly.

Stir in chicken, vegetables, and seasoning.

Prepare pie crust (bottom) according to package directions. Place in 9-inch deep pie plate. Spoon in chicken mixture.

Combine egg and water. Brush on edges of pie crust. Top with second pie crust and crimp edges. Cut slits in crust.

Bake 30 to 35 minutes or until golden brown and bubbly. Let stand 5 minutes before serving.

Yield: 6 to 8 servings.

Soups & Stews

Only the pure of heart can make a good soup.

Ludwig Van Beethoven

Conversation Starters

- A STATE OF MIND

  1. If you could live in any other state, which one would it be?

  2. Which state has the most mountains?

  3. Which state is known for its many lakes?

  4. Which state is known as the Tarheel State?

  5. Name at least five states with beaches.

- THE BACKWARDS MEAL

Remember this one from summer camp? Wear your clothes backwards, and eat your meal in backwards order. That's right, Mom. Dessert first.

- JUST SOUPER!

Next time you serve soup, try these questions:

  1. Who's your favorite super-hero?

  2. Who's your super friend?

  3. Can you name a real live super-hero? (a neighbor, helper, teacher, etc.)

Cool Gazpacho

3 large tomatoes, seeded and finely
   chopped
2 stalks celery, finely chopped
1 cucumber, seeded and finely chopped
1 clove garlic, minced
¼ cup red onion, finely chopped
1 tablespoon chopped fresh parsley
3 tablespoons tarragon or white wine
   vinegar
1 teaspoon salt
½ teaspoon pepper
4 cups tomato or tomato-vegetable juice

   Combine all ingredients in a large bowl (do
not use aluminum). Cover and chill several
hours.

Yield: 4 to 6 servings.

Herbed Gazpacho:
   Substitute chopped fresh basil or cilantro for
parsley.

*Per serving: 50 calories, 0.3 g. fat, 0 mg.
cholesterol, 669 mg. sodium*

This cool, refreshing
soup is the perfect
way to highlight
summer tomatoes.
For ease, chop
vegetables in a food
processor. For a
prettier presenta-
tion, finely chop the
ingredients by hand.

Golden Butternut Squash Soup

You can prepare this soup in advance and serve it hot or chilled. The soup tends to thicken as it cools, so you may need to add additional broth.

2 butternut squash, halved and seeded
2 tablespoons butter
2 cloves garlic, minced
1 onion, chopped
2 (16-ounce) cans fat-free chicken broth
½ teaspoon salt
Cracked black pepper (optional)

Preheat oven to 375°.

Place squash halves, cut side down, in a large roasting or baking pan. Add water to a depth of ½ inch. Bake for 45 to 60 minutes or until tender when pierced with a knife. Let cool; spoon out flesh, and set aside.

Melt butter in a large Dutch oven or soup pot over medium-high heat. Add garlic and onion; cook 3 to 5 minutes or until tender.

Stir reserved squash, broth and salt. Bring to a boil, reduce heat, and simmer 15 minutes.

Place one-third of mixture into container of blender, and blend until pureed. (Place kitchen towel over blender top to prevent hot liquid from splattering.) Repeat procedure with remaining squash mixture.

Serve immediately or chill. Sprinkle each serving with a small amount of black pepper, if desired.

Yield: 6 servings.

Per serving: 141 calories, 2.2 g. fat, 5 mg. cholesterol, 552 mg. sodium

Butternut squash are vividly colored winter squash. Can you name other bright orange gourds?

Potato-Cheese Soup

 kid friendly

This rich soup brightens a cold, rainy day.

4 slices bacon, cut into pieces
1 tablespoon olive oil
2 stalks celery, finely chopped
1 carrot, finely chopped
1 onion, finely chopped
3 tablespoons all-purpose flour
2 (16-ounce) cans fat-free chicken broth
3 large potatoes, peeled and diced
1 (16-ounce) package processed cheese
     loaf
1 teaspoon hot sauce
½ teaspoon Worcestershire sauce
1 cup half-and-half

Cook bacon over medium-high heat in a large soup pot until crispy. Remove bacon, and set aside.

Drain bacon grease reserving 1 tablespoon in pot. Add olive oil, celery, carrot, and onion. Cook 3 to 5 minutes or until tender.

Stir in flour; cook 1 minute.

Add chicken broth and potatoes. Bring to a boil; reduce heat, and simmer 20 minutes or until potatoes are tender.

Add cheese, hot sauce, and Worcestershire sauce, stirring until cheese is blended.

Stir in half-and-half; cook until hot. (Do not boil.) To serve, sprinkle with reserved bacon.

Yield: 6 servings.

Believe it or not, potatoes as well as tomatoes, were believed to be poisonous when they were introduced hundreds of years ago.

Slow-Simmered Bean Soup

Serve this "chill chaser" with hot, buttered cornbread.

2 slices bacon
1 onion, chopped
2 cloves garlic, minced
1 (19-ounce) can cannellini beans, undrained
1 (16-ounce) can chili beans, undrained
1 (15-ounce) can black beans, undrained
1 cup chopped cooked ham
1 (14.5-ounce) can stewed tomatoes
1 (16-ounce) can fat-free chicken broth
2 teaspoons grated lemon rind
2 tablespoons fresh lemon juice
2 bay leaves
Hot sauce

Cook bacon in a Dutch oven or large, tall pot over medium heat until crisp. Remove bacon; crumble and set aside.

Add onion and garlic. Cook over medium heat 1 minute or until tender. Add beans, chopped ham, tomatoes, broth, rind, juice, and bay leaves.

Bring to a boil; reduce heat to medium-low and cook 30 minutes, stirring occasionally.

Cook until soup is desired consistency. (Cooking longer will make it thicker; removing it from heat immediately will make the soup thinner.) Remove bay leaves, and serve with hot sauce.

Yield: 4 to 6 servings.

Note: The lemon will yield more juice if you microwave the whole fruit at HIGH for 30 seconds, and then roll it around on the countertop just before you slice it.

Chicken and Cheddar Cheese Dumplings

1 (3- to 4-pound) whole chicken, cut up
3 tablespoons olive oil
3 carrots, sliced
2 stalks celery, sliced
1 onion, chopped
1 teaspoon herb seasoning for chicken
    or poultry seasoning
1 teaspoon salt
1 teaspoon pepper
2 (16-ounce) cans chicken broth
1½ cups all-purpose flour
2 teaspoons baking powder
1 teaspoon salt
1 tablespoon chopped fresh parsley
3 tablespoons butter, cut into pieces
½ cup milk
¼ cup sour cream
¼ cup shredded Cheddar cheese

Remove large pieces of skin from chicken. Brown chicken in olive oil in a large Dutch oven or soup pot over medium heat. Drain oil, if desired.

Add carrots, celery, onion, seasoning, salt, and pepper; stir in broth. Bring mixture to a boil, cover, reduce heat, and simmer 45 minutes or until chicken is tender. Remove chicken, reserving broth.

Combine flour, baking powder, salt, and parsley. Cut in butter with a pastry blender or fork. Stir in milk, sour cream, and cheese. Drop tablespoons of dumpling batter into hot broth. Cover and simmer 15 minutes.

Remove chicken from bones; gently stir chicken into dumpling mixture.

Yield: 4 to 6 servings.

Dumpling is a euphemism given to loved ones. Can you think of other food terms of endearment?

Homemade Chicken Noodle Soup

1 (3-pound) broiler-fryer chicken
1 tablespoon olive oil
8½ cups water, divided
1 onion, chopped
2 stalks celery, sliced
1 clove garlic, minced
1½ teaspoons salt, divided
6 ounces spaghetti
2 carrots, peeled and sliced
½ teaspoon dried rosemary
½ teaspoon dried basil
½ teaspoon ground sage
½ teaspoon pepper
2 bay leaves

Remove large pieces of skin from chicken. Brown chicken on breast and back in olive oil in a large Dutch oven or soup pot over medium heat.

Add 3½ cups water. Stir in onion, celery, garlic, and ½ teaspoon salt. Cover and cook 30 minutes over medium heat.

Remove chicken from pot and pull chicken from bone. (Use a fork or wear rubber gloves to protect fingers from burning.) Chop chicken into bite-size pieces, and return meat to pot.

Add remaining 5 cups water, spaghetti, carrots, 1 teaspoon salt, rosemary, basil, sage, pepper, and bay leaves. Bring to a boil. Reduce heat to medium-low, and cook 20 minutes. Remove bay leaves before serving.

Yield: 6 servings.

Note: For a healthy make-ahead soup: Follow directions and refrigerate. A little fat will congeal on top of soup. Remove fat. The noodles thicken the soup when it sits, so add water to reheat it.

Per serving: 346 calories, 10.3 g. fat, 93 mg. cholesterol, 643 mg. sodium

Cajun Seafood Soup

By adding 1 to 3 tablespoons Cajun Seasoning Blend, you can determine how spicy to make your soup.

¼ cup butter
4 green onions, chopped
3 stalks celery, chopped
1 green bell pepper, chopped
1 clove garlic, minced
1½ tablespoons Cajun Seasoning Blend (page 178)
1 (15-ounce) can tomato sauce
1 (14.5-ounce) can diced tomatoes
2 (16-ounce) cans fat-free chicken broth
1 pound mild white fish
1 pound medium shrimp, peeled and deveined
½ pound flaked crabmeat or imitation crabmeat

Melt butter in a large soup pot. Add green onions, celery, bell pepper, and garlic. Cook over medium-high heat 5 minutes.

Stir in Cajun Seasoning Blend, tomato sauce, and diced tomatoes. Cook 5 minutes.

Add broth, and simmer 15 minutes.

Stir in fish and seafood, and cook 5 minutes or until done.

Yield: 8 servings.

Per serving: 268 calories, 8.0 g. fat, 148 mg. cholesterol, 677 mg. sodium

Cajun Chicken Soup:
If you are not a seafood lover, simply substitute 6 skinned and boneless chicken breast halves, cut into strips. Simmer an additional 5 minutes or until chicken is tender.

How many stories, books, movies, etc. can your family name that involve fishing or seafood?

Smoked Turkey-Pasta Soup

Orzo, a rice-shaped pasta, adds nice texture to this soup. You may also use leftover roast turkey for this recipe.

1 tablespoon olive oil
3 carrots, chopped
3 stalks celery, chopped
1 onion, chopped
2 teaspoons chicken-herb seasoning or poultry seasoning
2 (16-ounce) cans fat-free chicken broth
1 (14.5-ounce) can no-salt-added diced tomatoes
½ cup orzo or other small pasta
2 cups chopped cooked smoked turkey

Heat olive oil in a large Dutch oven or soup pot over medium-high heat. Add carrots, celery, and onion and cook 5 minutes until tender.

Stir in seasoning, broth, tomatoes, orzo, and turkey; bring to a boil, reduce heat and simmer 20 minutes or until pasta is tender.

Yield: 6 servings.

Per serving: 268 calories, 8.1 g. fat, 54 mg. cholesterol, 411 mg. sodium

Quick Italian Beef Soup

Keep all the ingredients for this soup in the freezer or pantry for a spur-of-the-moment meal.

1   pound lean ground beef
4   cups water
3   beef bouillon cubes
1   (28-ounce) can fresh-cut tomatoes
1   (1-pound) package frozen sugar snap
      peas
4   ounces uncooked sea-shell or other
      small pasta
1½ tablespoons dried Italian seasoning
¼   teaspoon salt

   Brown ground beef in a large Dutch oven or soup pot, over medium-high heat, 3 to 5 minutes (or until meat is no longer pink), crumbling with a wooden spoon; drain.

   Add water and bouillon cubes. Add tomatoes, sugar snap peas, pasta, Italian seasoning, and salt. Bring to a boil. Reduce heat to medium, and simmer gently 15 minutes. Add water if a thinner soup is desired.

Yield: 6 to 8 servings.

This soup features the colors of the Italian flag: red, white, and green. Can you get all three colors on your spoon?

Quick Vegetable Soup

2 tablespoons butter

2 cloves garlic, minced

1 (16-ounce) package frozen Italian-style
vegetables

2 cups frozen hash brown potatoes

1 (15-ounce) can chunky Italian style
tomato sauce

1 (16-ounce) can fat-free chicken broth

Melt butter in a large Dutch oven or soup pot. Add garlic and cook 2 minutes or until lightly browned. Stir in remaining ingredients.

Bring mixture to a boil; reduce heat, and simmer 15 minutes.

Yield: 4 servings.

Per serving: 108 calories, 3.4 g. fat, 8 mg. cholesterol, 602 mg. sodium

■ ■ ■ ■ ■ ■ ■ ■ ■

Quick and heart-healthy, you might rename this flavorful recipe "lifesaver soup."

Black and White Bean Chili

1 tablespoon vegetable oil
2 cloves garlic, minced
1 onion, chopped
1 red bell pepper, chopped
1 green or yellow bell pepper, chopped
2 tablespoons all-purpose flour
1½ tablespoons Mexican Seasoning Blend (page 178)
2 (16-ounce) cans fat-free chicken broth
2 (15.8-ounce) Great Northern Beans, rinsed and drained
2 (15-ounce) cans black beans, rinsed and drained
½ cup shredded Monterey Jack cheese

Heat oil in a large Dutch oven over medium-high heat; add garlic, onion, and bell peppers. Cook 3 to 5 minutes or until tender. Stir in flour and seasoning blend; cook 1 minute.

Add broth and beans; cook 10 minutes or until thoroughly heated. Top each serving with cheese.

Yield: 8 servings.

Note: 1½ tablespoons taco seasoning mix can be substituted for Mexican blend.

Per serving: 334 calories, 4.9 g. fat, 6 mg. cholesterol, 988 mg. sodium

Black and White Bean Chicken Chili:
Add 2 cups chopped grilled chicken for an "outdoorsy" flavor.

Do you know how Monterey Jack cheese got its name? It was created in Monterey, California. Gorgonzola, Stilton, Cheddar, and Gloucester are a few more named after their hometown. Can you think of any other foods labeled after their city or country of origin?

Southwestern Chili Bean Pot

If you want more heat, stir in a fresh chopped jalapeño pepper. To tame heat, top chili with a dollop of sour cream.

1 pound lean ground beef
1 green bell pepper, chopped
1 onion, chopped
1 (30-ounce) can chili hot beans, undrained
1 (14.5-ounce) can no-salt-added stewed tomatoes
1 (6-ounce) can tomato paste
1 tablespoon chili powder
2 teaspoons ground cumin
1 teaspoon cocoa
¼ teaspoon ground cinnamon
Sour Cream, shredded cheese, hot sauce

Brown ground beef in a large Dutch oven over medium-high heat, stirring until meat crumbles and is no longer pink. Add bell pepper and onion. Cook, stirring occasionally, until vegetables are tender, about 3 to 5 minutes.

Add beans, tomatoes, tomato paste chili powder, cumin, cocoa, and cinnamon. Bring to a boil. Reduce heat and simmer, uncovered, 30 minutes. Cover and cook 45 minutes to 1 hour, stirring occasionally. Serve with sour cream, cheese, and hot sauce.

Yield: 6 servings.

Slow Cooker Chili:
Brown ground beef in a nonstick skillet over medium-high heat. Add to 4-quart slow cooker. Add bell pepper, onion, beans (for slow cooker, drain beans), tomatoes, tomato paste, chili powder, cumin, cocoa, and cinnamon. Stir well. Cover and cook on HIGH 3 to 4 hours or LOW 6 to 8 hours.

South O' the Border Pork Stew

1½-2 pounds (½-inch thick) boneless center cut pork loin chops
1 tablespoon chili powder
2 (15-ounce) cans black beans, undrained
1 (16-ounce) can fat-free chicken broth
1 (14.5-ounce) can stewed tomatoes
1 (11-ounce) can kernel corn, drained
2 (4-ounce) cans chopped green chiles
1 medium onion, sliced
2 cloves garlic, minced
1 teaspoon cumin
½ teaspoon dried oregano

Cut pork chops into 1-inch pieces, and place in a bowl or zip-top plastic bag. Add chili powder and toss to coat.

Coat a nonstick skillet with vegetable cooking spray and place over medium-high heat. Cook pork, stirring frequently, about 3 minutes, until browned.

Transfer pork to a large Dutch oven. Add black beans, broth, tomatoes, corn, chiles, onion, garlic, cumin, and oregano. Cook over medium-low heat, covered, for 45 minutes. Uncover and cook 15 to 30 minutes.

Yield: 8 to 10 servings.

Slow Cooker Border Stew:
Brown pork as directed; transfer to a 4-quart slow cooker. Add black beans, broth , tomatoes, corn, chiles, onion, garlic, cumin, and oregano. Cook on HIGH 3 to 4 hours or LOW 6 to 8 hours. Combine 3 tablespoons flour with ¼ cup cold water, stirring well with a fork. Add to pork mixture; cover and cook 30 more minutes.

Take advantage of this recipe when boneless pork chops are on sale. Tossing the pork cubes with chile powder imparts flavor and adds warmth to this recipe.

Pot Roast with Pizzazz

Tired of the same old pot roast? Try this one, inspired by cooking teacher Richard Grausman. If you've never used fresh ginger or ground coriander, you'll be amazed at the vitality they add to the dish.

Gingerroot looks like a mutant flower bulb. It's known for its pungency and aroma. Look for gingerroot that is plump and unwrinkled. Peel the tough brown skin before mincing or grating.

2 tablespoons vegetable oil
1 (2½- to 3-pound) boneless beef roast (see note on page 92)
1 tablespoon vegetable oil
2 onions, sliced into ¼-inch rings
4 carrots, peeled and cut into 2-inch pieces
3 tablespoons all-purpose flour
1 (10¾-ounce) can tomato soup
2⅔ cups water
2 beef bouillon cubes
1 inch fresh gingerroot, very thinly sliced
2 cloves garlic, minced
3 teaspoons ground coriander
12-14 small red potatoes, cut in half

Brown roast in 2 tablespoons oil in a Dutch oven pot over medium heat, 2 minutes on each side. Remove meat and set aside.

Add 1 tablespoon oil, onion rings, and carrots. Cook, uncovered, 5 to 7 minutes, stirring occasionally, until browned.

Add flour. Cook, uncovered, stirring frequently, 3 minutes. Add tomato soup, water, bouillon, ginger, garlic, and coriander.

Return meat to mixture, and cook, covered, at medium low heat 1½ hours. Add potatoes and cook, covered, and additional hour.

To serve, remove meat and vegetables. Simmer cooking juices 10 minutes to reduce sauce. Slice meat and arrange with vegetables on platter. Serve with reduced juices from pan.

Yield: 6 servings.

Note: 1 teaspoon ground ginger or 1 teaspoon allspice may be substituted for fresh gingerroot.

Slow Cooker Pot Roast with Pizzazz:

Brown roast as directed. Place in slow cooker. Add onions, carrots, and potatoes. Combine tomato soup, gingerroot, garlic, bouillon cubes, and coriander; stir well and pour over vegetables. (Do not add oil, water, or flour.) Cover and cook on HIGH 3 to 4 hours or LOW 6 to 8 hours.

■ ■ ■ ■ ■ ■ ■ ■ ■

Whether cooked in a Dutch oven or slow cooker, this pot roast needs browning as a first step. Browning adds color and flavor.

Picante Pot Roast

For a satisfying meal, slice roast; add back to pot, and serve over Quick Cheese Grits (page 132) or rice.

1 (2½ to 3-pound) boneless beef roast
1 tablespoon vegetable oil
1 (12-ounce) bottle of beer
3 tablespoons brown sugar (optional)
1 (16-ounce) jar picante sauce or 2 cups salsa

Trim visible fat from roast. Brown roast in oil in a large Dutch oven over medium heat, about 3 minutes on each side.

Add beer, brown sugar, and picante sauce. Bring to a boil. Cover, reduce heat and simmer 2 hours.

Yield: 4 to 6 servings.

Slow Cooker Picante Pot Roast:
Brown roast as directed and place in slow cooker. Add 1 cup beer, sugar (if desired), and 1½ cups salsa. Cover and cook on HIGH 3 to hours or LOW 6 to 8 hours.

While chuck roasts are probably the most frequently chosen beef cut for pot roasts, leaner cuts such as sirloin tip roasts, brisket, and English roasts (or shoulder roasts) are also candidates. The secret to tender pot roast is to gently cook, covered, in flavorful liquid for at least 2 hours. If you use a roast with the words "loin" or "round" in it, you have a roast with less fat.

Grilling

Laughter is brightest where
food is best.

Irish Proverb

Conversation Starters

- **YOU DESERVE A HUG**

  Before everyone sits down to dinner, host a hug-a-thon. No one sits down until they've hugged everyone at the table.

- **COLOR ME CRAZY**

  You'll think you're back at camp when you eat dinner by color—green items first, brown second, red third, etc.

- **JOKE OF THE DAY**

  Ask your family to bring a new joke to tell at the table. Here's one you can use: "Did you hear about the new restaurant on the moon? It's got great food, but no atmosphere!"

Pepper-Steak Kabobs

Kabobs offer a fun way to cook and serve a grilled meal. If you are using wooden skewers, soak them in water at least 30 minutes before adding meat and vegetables.

¼ cup soy sauce
1 teaspoon sesame oil
¼ cup firmly packed brown sugar
1 teaspoon chili paste with garlic (optional)
½ large red onion, cut into 2-inch pieces
2 green bell peppers, cut into 2-inch pieces
1 pound sirloin steak, cut into 2-inch cubes
1 (8-ounce) package fresh mushrooms

Combine soy sauce, sesame oil, brown sugar, and, if desired, chili paste in a large zip-top plastic bag or shallow dish.

Add vegetables and steak, tossing to coat; cover and chill several hours or overnight.

Thread meat and vegetables on metal or wooden skewers, discarding marinade.

Grill kabobs over medium-hot (350° to 400°) coals 10 minutes, or until to desired doneness, turning once. Serve with hot, cooked rice.

Yield: 4 to 6 servings.

Wonder why your kabobs are almost always tan color throughout, even when you try to grill them medium-rare? It's the acid in the marinade that browns and tenderizes.

Best Burger Bets

Few things are as good as a burger hot off the grill. These variations make it even more fun to cook out. Once your creative juices start flowing, you're likely to come up with your own combinations. We've left room for you to jot those down, too.

Burger Basics:

Use your choice of ground beef, turkey, chicken, pork, or a combination of these meats. For testing, we shaped meat into ⅛-pound patties, spread the filling on one patty, and topped it with another to make a ¼-pound burger with filling. For gooey, cheesy fillings, be sure to pinch the patties together all the way around so the filling won't leak.

Time It Right:

Grilling times ranged from 5 to 7 minutes on each side. Burgers with fillings are sometimes tough to gauge for doneness. To be on the safe side, completely cut one burger open and be sure meat is cooked through.

The Trimmings:

For some burgers, we've offered tips on how to top them once they come off the grill. You can toast the buns on the grill, too.

Blue Cheese Burgers:

Spoon 1½ tablespoons crumbled blue cheese in center of patty; top with another patty and grill.

Pimiento Cheese Burgers:

Spread one patty with 2 tablespoons commercial pimiento cheese; top with another, patty and grill.

Roasted Garlic Burgers:

Add ¾ cup oats and ¼ cup steak sauce to 1 pound ground meat. Spoon 1 to 2 tablespoons light roasted garlic-flavored cream cheese on top of a patty; top with another patty and grill.

kid friendly

Make sure ground beef is cooked until no pink remains, especially if you are cooking for children, pregnant woman, or the elderly (their immune systems are weaker). Bacteria, present on cut surfaces, is stirred in when meat is ground. (Thus they need to cook well done.) Larger cuts of beef have few cut surfaces. That is why you can cook steaks rare, or medium-rare.

South O' The Border Burger:

Sprinkle 1½ tablespoons shredded Monterey Jack cheese with peppers in center of patty; top with another patty, and grill. Serve burger with salsa.

The Frenchmen's Burgers:

Add ¼ cup Dijon mustard and 2 teaspoons capers to 1 pound ground meat. Shape into ¼-pound patties, and grill. Top each with 1 slice Gruyère or Swiss cheese.

Onion-Topped Burgers:

Slice two Vidalia or other sweet onions into rings. Let stand in a pool of balsamic vinegar at least 30 minutes, stirring occasionally. Place rings in a grilling basket and grill over medium heat (300° to 350°) until onions are dark brown around the edges, turning at least once. Toss grilled onions with 1 teaspoon vinegar and 1 teaspoon olive oil; add salt and pepper to taste. Serve on burgers.

Port Wine Picnic Burgers:

Purchase a port wine cheese ball at the supermarket or deli. (We like the ones coated with nuts.) Cut a ¼-inch slice through the center of the cheese ball and lay it on top of an ⅛-pound patty making sure the patty is larger than the cheese slice. Top with another patty, sealing well. Repeat with more ground beef and the rest of the cheese ball. Amounts will vary due to shape of the cheese ball; grill.

Sweet Cola Chops

With only four ingredients, this fat-free, fizzy marinade partners well with chicken, pork, and beef.

1 cup diet or regular cola beverage
½ cup ketchup
¼ cup Worcestershire sauce
1 teaspoon garlic powder
8 (1-inch-thick) boneless pork chops

Combine cola, ketchup, Worcestershire sauce, and garlic powder in a zip-top plastic bag or shallow dish. Reserve ¼ cup marinade for basting. Add pork chops, tossing to coat; cover and chill several hours or overnight. Remove chops, discarding marinade. Coat grill rack with vegetable cooking spray. Grill chops with lid closed over medium-hot (350° to 400°) coals, 4 to 5 minutes. Brush with reserved marinade; turn and brush again. Grill, covered, 4 to 5 minutes or until center of chop is slightly pink.

Yield: 8 servings.

Balsamic-Dijon Lamb Chops

¼ cup balsamic vinegar
¼ cup Dijon mustard
1 clove garlic, minced
½ teaspoon chopped fresh rosemary
4 (1-inch-thick) lamb shoulder chops

Combine vinegar, mustard, garlic, and rosemary in a zip-top plastic bag or shallow dish. Add lamb chops, tossing to coat; cover and chill at least 30 minutes. Remove chops, discarding marinade. Coat grill rack with vegetable cooking spray. Grill chops with lid closed over medium (300° to 350°) coals 10 to 12 minutes, turning once.

Yield: 4 servings.

When grilling, the coals should not flame. Wait until the coals are white-hot; otherwise, flare-ups will char foods and produce distasteful smoke.

This versatile, fat-free marinade also works well for beef, chicken or pork. Pair this dish with a hearty Cabernet Sauvignon wine.

Honey-Glazed Pork Tenderloin

Paired with Sweet Potato Rolls (page 171), this delectable pork makes excellent finger sandwiches.

½ cup olive oil and vinegar salad dressing
¼ cup soy sauce
¼ cup honey
1¾ pound pork tenderloin, trimmed

Combine salad dressing, soy sauce, and honey in a large zip-top bag or shallow dish.

Add pork, tossing to coat; cover and chill several hours or overnight.

Remove pork from marinade, discarding marinade.

Grill pork with lid closed over medium-hot (350° to 400°) coals 15 to 20 minutes or until meat thermometer registers 150°, turning once.

Yield: 4 to 6 servings.

Gone are the days when pork had to be cooked to a dry, tasteless gray. It's actually preferable to see a slightly pink center (proof that it's juicy).

kid friendly

BBQ Ham Steak

Buy the small, 6-pack cans of pineapple juice to keep on hand for recipes such as this. You can also toss a can with cut fruit to keep it from browning.

1 cup pineapple juice
3 tablespoons butter, melted
½ cup firmly packed brown sugar
½ teaspoon ground cloves
¼ teaspoon dry mustard
⅓ cup dry sherry (optional)
1 (1½-pound) center-cut ham steak
   (about ½-inch thick)

Combine juice, butter, brown sugar, cloves, mustard, and, if desired, sherry in a plastic zip-top bag or shallow dish.

Add ham, tossing to coat; cover and chill several hours or overnight.

Grill ham with lid open over medium-high (350° to 400°) coals, 5 minutes on each side, basting frequently.

Yield: 4 servings.

Year-round grilling is popular for many people. But when the mercury drops, so does the temperature of your grill. You may need to increase grilling time to thoroughly cook food.

Asian Grill

This marinade also works well with a whole cut-up chicken or leg and thigh quarters.

¾ cup crunchy peanut butter
¼ cup lime or lemon juice
¼ cup light soy sauce
¼ cup firmly packed brown sugar
¼ teaspoon minced garlic
¼-½ teaspoon red or cayenne pepper
6 boneless chicken breasts

Combine peanut butter, juice, soy sauce, brown sugar, garlic, and pepper in a zip-top plastic bag or shallow dish. Reserve ½ cup marinade to use later as sauce

Add chicken, tossing to coat. Cover and chill 30 minutes or overnight.

Remove chicken, discarding marinade. Coat grill rack with vegetable cooking spray.

Grill chicken with lid closed over medium-hot (350° to 400°) coals 5 minutes on each side or until done. Serve with reserved sauce.

Yield: 6 servings.

Asian Flank Steak:
Combine marinade ingredients; reserve ½ cup marinade to use later as sauce. Cut a crisscross pattern on top of 1½- to 2- pound flank steak; add to marinade. Cover and chill as directed. Coat grill rack with vegetable cooking spray. Grill steak with grill lid opened over medium (300° to 350°) coals 17 to 21 minutes, turning once. Serve with reserved sauce.

Ask your family if they can identify the secret ingredient in this marinade (kitchen helpers will have to vow silence!) It's peanut butter.

Balsamic Barbecued Chicken

½ cup barbecue sauce
½ cup balsamic vinegar
1 teaspoon garlic powder
8 boneless chicken breasts

Combine barbecue sauce, vinegar, and garlic powder in a zip-top plastic bag or shallow dish. (If you are making Barbecued Chicken Salad, reserve ¼ cup of marinade to make salad dressing.)

Add chicken, tossing to coat, cover and chill least one hour or overnight.

Remove chicken, discarding marinade. Coat grill rack with vegetable cooking spray.

Grill chicken with lid closed over medium-hot (350° to 400°) coals 5 minutes on each side or until done.

Yield: 8 servings.

Barbecued Chicken Salad:

Toss together 1 (16-ounce) can pinto beans, rinsed and drained; 1 (10-ounce) bag romaine salad greens; 2 cups sliced carrots; 2 tomatoes, chopped; 2 stalks celery, sliced; and 1 cucumber, sliced.

To serve:

Cut barbecued chicken breasts into long strips. (You'll have about four to five strips from each breast.) Place salad in the center of a large dinner plate. Arrange chicken strips in a starburst pattern on the greens. Spoon Warm Corn-Balsamic Vinaigrette over the top of the chicken.

Warm Corn-Balsamic Vinaigrette:

Combine reserved ¼ cup chicken marinade, 1½ tablespoons balsamic vinegar, 3 tablespoons water, and 3 tablespoons olive oil in a small saucepan. Stir in 1 (2-ounce) jar chopped pimientos, drained and 1 (15.25-ounce) can corn kernels, drained. Heat 2 to 3 minutes or until bubbly.

BBQ Chicken with White-Pepper Sauce

1   cup mayonnaise
3   tablespoons apple cider vinegar
3   tablespoons sour cream
2   tablespoons lemon juice
1   tablespoon vegetable oil
2   teaspoons coarsely ground black
      pepper
1   teaspoon sugar
6   boneless chicken breasts

Combine mayonnaise, vinegar, sour cream, lemon juice, oil, pepper, and sugar in a small bowl.

Place chicken breasts in a zip-top plastic bag or shallow dish; add ½ cup sauce, tossing to coat. Cover and chill 30 minutes.

Remove chicken, discarding marinade. Coat grill rack with vegetable cooking spray. Grill chicken with lid closed over medium (300° to 350°) coals 15 minutes or until done, turning once. Serve with remaining sauce.

Yield: 6 servings.

Note: You may substitute a whole cut up chicken, a "pick-of-the-chick" package, or leg and thigh quarters; remove large pieces of skin.

This unique sauce enhances freshly steamed vegetables, too.

Pineapple-Chicken Melt

1 (8-ounce) can pineapple slices
½ cup soy sauce
¼ cup dry sherry or pineapple juice
2 tablespoons rice or white wine vinegar
2 tablespoons fresh minced gingerroot
2 cloves garlic, minced
4 boneless chicken breasts
4 slices Provolone cheese
4 onion or club rolls, split
Mayonnaise, lettuce (optional)

Drain pineapple, reserving juice for marinade, if desired. Set aside.

Combine soy sauce, sherry (or juice), vinegar, gingerroot, and garlic in a zip-top plastic bag or shallow bowl.

Add chicken, tossing to coat; cover and chill at least 1 hour.

Remove chicken, discarding marinade. Coat grill rack with vegetable cooking spray.

Grill chicken with lid closed over medium-hot (350° to 400°) coals 5 minutes on each side or until done.

Place one pineapple slice and one cheese slice over each breast. Cover and grill 1 minute until cheese slightly melts; set aside.

Grill rolls until toasted. Spread bottom half with mayonnaise and top with lettuce, if desired. Add chicken and top half of roll.

Yield: 4 servings.

Grilled Marinated Turkey Breast

⅓ cup fresh orange juice
2 tablespoons fresh lemon juice
2 tablespoons fresh lime juice
¼ cup olive oil
1 teaspoon pepper
½ teaspoon salt
1 (6-pound) turkey breast, split in half

Combine juices, olive oil, pepper, and salt.

Place turkey in large, zip-top plastic bag or shallow dish. Carefully pull skin away from breast meat forming a pocket under skin. Pour marinade over turkey and under skin to trap marinade next to meat. Cover and chill several hours or overnight.

Remove turkey, discarding marinade. Grill turkey with lid closed over medium-hot (350° to 400°) coals 15 to 20 minutes, or until done, turning once.

Yield: 12 servings.

Note: It takes a very sharp knife or scissors and arm strength to divide the turkey breast in half. Smile and ask the folks behind the meat counter to do it for you.

Per serving: 307 calories, 11.7 g. fat, 86 mg. cholesterol, 915 mg. sodium

■ ■ ■ ■ ■ ■ ■ ■

If you've never grilled turkey, this recipe is reason enough to start. Serve it with Cranberry Salsa on page 175.

■ ■ ■ ■ ■ ■ ■ ■

Chili-Grilled Shark Steaks

Any variety fish will swim with this quick marinade, including tuna, halibut, grouper, catfish, and amberjack.

2 tablespoons fresh lemon juice
2 tablespoons olive oil
½ teaspoon garlic powder
½ teaspoon chili powder
⅛ teaspoon pepper
1½ pounds shark steaks
  (¾- to 1-inch thick)

Combine lemon juice, olive oil, garlic powder, chili powder, and pepper in a zip-top plastic bag or shallow dish.

Add fish, tossing to coat. Let stand 20 to 30 minutes (longer marinating will make the fish mushy).

Remove fish, discarding marinade. Coat grill rack with vegetable cooking spray.

Grill fish with lid closed over medium (300° to 350°) coals 7 minutes; turn fish and grill additional 3 to 4 minutes.

Yield: 4 servings.

Note: Recipe may be doubled. Six ounces of fish feeds one person. This recipe stands alone nicely, or pair it with a salsa from the Good Stuff chapter.

Chili-Grilled Fish Sandwich:

Stir together ½ cup commercial tartar sauce and ¼ teaspoon chili powder. Use this in place of mayonnaise for your sandwich. Spread on toasted buns; top with fish, fresh tomatoes, and lettuce. Serve with fresh lemon wedges and chips.

Marinated Grilled Vegetables

Be sure to cut the vegetables into large pieces or use a grill basket. You don't want to lose any to the hot coals below.

⅓ cup balsamic vinegar
2 tablespoons olive oil
2 tablespoons molasses
1 teaspoon chopped fresh basil
1 teaspoon chopped fresh oregano
1 teaspoon chopped fresh thyme
½ teaspoon salt
½ teaspoon pepper
4 carrots, halved and cut into 3-inch pieces
3 zucchini, sliced diagonally
3 yellow squash, sliced diagonally
1 onion, quartered and separated into pieces

Combine vinegar, oil, molasses, herbs, salt, and pepper in a zip-top plastic bag or shallow dish.

Add vegetables, tossing to coat. Cover and let stand at least 30 minutes.

Remove vegetables, reserving marinade. Grill over medium-hot (350° to 400°) coals 5 to 8 minutes or until vegetables are tender, turning once. (Remove vegetables as they cook to avoid burning.)

Toss vegetables with reserved marinade, and serve.

Yield: 6 servings

Per serving: 112 calories, 4.9 g. fat, 0 mg. cholesterol, 201 mg. sodium

Grilled Vegetable Salad:
Prepare recipe as directed. Cover vegetables and refrigerate until chilled. Toss with 3 ounces goat cheese or feta cheese, and serve on a bed of mixed baby greens.

Why are dull knives more dangerous than sharp ones? Dull knives require more pressure to cut or slice, and therefore are more likely to slip. To keep your knives sharp, use a wood or white polyethylene cutting board, and never wash them in the dishwasher.

Grilled Chicken Quesadilla

■ ■ ■ ■ ■ ■ ■ ■ ■

If you're scared of flipping tortillas on the grill, try this tip: Transfer tortillas to a plate, cover with another plate, flip, and then return to the grill.

2 tablespoons lime juice
1 tablespoon olive oil
1 tablespoon Mexican Seasoning Blend (page 178)
3 large, boneless chicken breasts
8 8-inch flour tortillas
1 cup Mexican-style shredded cheese blend

Combine lime juice, oil, and seasoning in a zip-top plastic bag or shallow dish.

Add chicken, tossing to coat; cover and chill 30 minutes.

Remove chicken, discarding marinade. Grill chicken with lid closed over medium-hot (350° to 400°) coals 5 minutes on each side or until done.

Let cool enough to handle; slice into ¼-inch strips.

Lay 4 tortillas on a flat surface; spread evenly with chicken and cheese. Top with remaining tortillas.

Grill uncovered over medium-hot coals 2 to 3 minutes or until toasted, turning once. Cut into quarters, and serve with any of the salsas in the Good Stuff chapter.

Yield: 4 servings or 8 appetizer servings.

Note: 1 teaspoon ground cumin can be substituted for Mexican blend.

No Forks Necessary

Cooking is like love.
It should be entered into with
abandon or not at all.

Harriet Van Horne

Conversation Starters

- **NAME THAT PLACE**

Use maps for innovative place mats. You can pick them up at restaurants, photocopy them from books, or cut them out of an old paperback atlas. Have more time? Cut maps into pieces and laminate them. After supper, ask the kids to piece them together like a puzzle

- **A REAL PAGE-TURNER**

Use these questions to encourage table talk.

1. What's the best book you've read recently?

2. If you could be any character in a book, who would it be?

3. What's the neatest thing you've discovered in a book?

Roasted Chicken and Potato Pizza

½ cup commercial Alfredo sauce
1 (12-inch) prepared pizza crust
1 medium potato, baked, chilled, and sliced
1 teaspoon chopped fresh rosemary
2 cups chopped cooked chicken
½ cup shredded Monterey Jack cheese

Preheat oven to 400°.

Spread Alfredo over crust. Place potato slices evenly on pizza; sprinkle with rosemary. Top with chicken and cheese.

Bake for 15 minutes or until cheese melts.

Yield: 2 to 4 servings.

To make this a 30-minute meal, bake an extra potato when you roast a whole chicken. No one will suspect you transformed leftovers when you serve this quick and easy recipe.

Mediterranean-Tomato Pizza

3 large tomatoes, thinly sliced
1 (12-inch) prepared pizza crust
½ cup crumbled feta cheese
½ cup Greek black cured olives, pitted and coarsely chopped
½ cup shredded mozzarella cheese
1 tablespoon olive oil

Preheat oven to 375°.

Arrange tomato slices on top of crust, overlapping edges. Top with feta cheese, olives, and mozzarella cheese. Drizzle with olive oil.

Bake for 15 minutes or until golden brown and thoroughly heated.

Yield: 2 to 4 servings.

Note: To pit olives, crush them under the flat blade of a large knife and remove the pits with your fingers.

This sauceless pizza is an interesting variation of the standard pie. For added taste, try one of the flavored feta cheeses available.

Quick Fajita Skillet

Use chicken tenderloins, and you won't have to cut up chicken breasts.

Fajitas (pronounced Fah-HEE-tahs), is a favorite recipe from the American Southwest and Mexico. It celebrates regional ingredients such as tomatoes, tortillas (the Southwest version of bread), and cilantro. Ask your kids: If someone were celebrating their region of the country what dish would they tell them to make?

1 tablespoon vegetable oil
1 clove garlic, minced
1 pound chicken tenderloins
1 small onion, sliced
1 medium green bell pepper, sliced into rings
¼ cup reduced-sodium soy sauce
1 teaspoon Mexican Seasoning Blend (page 178)
2 tablespoons fresh lime juice
1 medium tomato, coarsely chopped
1-2 tablespoons chopped fresh cilantro (optional)
Warm flour tortillas
Sour cream
Guacamole

Heat oil in a large nonstick skillet over medium heat. Add garlic; cook 1 minute, stirring constantly. Add chicken, onion, bell pepper, soy sauce, and seasoning blend. Cook 3 minutes, stirring constantly.

Add lime juice and tomato to chicken mixture; cook until thoroughly heated. Stir in cilantro, if desired.

Serve from skillet at the table. Wrap the chicken mixture in warmed tortillas, and serve with sour cream and guacamole, if desired.

Yield: 4 servings.

Note: ½ teaspoon ground cumin can be substituted for Mexican blend.

Tortilla Rolls

4 ounces (½ cup) Neufchâtel light cream
   cheese, softened
1 tablespoon Mexican Seasoning Blend
   (page 178)
6 (8-inch) flour tortillas
2 cups fresh spinach leaves
1 large roasted bell pepper, sliced
1 large ripe avocado, sliced
1 cup spicy sprouts or alfalfa sprouts

Combine cream cheese with Mexican
Seasoning Blend; spread evenly on 1 side of
tortillas. Place spinach, roasted pepper,
avocado, and sprouts on cream cheese mixture.

Roll tortillas, securing with a wooden pick.
Serve with Almost Fresh Salsa (page 173).

Yield: 6 servings.

*Per serving: 227 calories, 11.1 g. fat, 11 mg.
cholesterol, 454 mg. sodium*

Note: Add grilled shrimp or sliced chicken
breasts to rolls for a more filling sandwich.
Appetizer idea: Cut tortillas into 1½-inch pieces,
and secure with a wooden pick.

A ripe avocado
yields to light
pressure (most sold
in grocery stores are
hard). To ripen,
place avocado in a
paper sack at room
temperature for a
couple of days. Ripe
avocados can be
refrigerated for
several days.

English Muffulettas

6 English muffins
Creole mustard
Mayonnaise
1 cup Olive Salad
6 slices Provolone cheese
6 slices smoked turkey
6 slices ham
6 slices salami

Muffulettas are a favorite New Orleans sandwich. This version uses English muffins instead of round Italian bread.

Preheat oven to 350°.

Split muffins and toast lightly. Spread halves with mustard and mayonnaise.

Spoon Olive Salad evenly over 6 halves. Top with cheese, meats, and remaining muffin halves.

Bake sandwiches 3 to 5 minutes until hot.

Yield: 6 servings.

Olive Salad:
1 cup green olives with pimientos
1 cup pitted ripe olives
1 cup pickled mixed vegetables
2 tablespoons olive oil
1 clove garlic
1 teaspoon Italian seasoning

Combine ingredients in bowl of electric food processor. Pulse several times until finely chopped. Cover tightly and store in refrigerator.

Yield: 3 cups.

Pizzeria-Style Chicken Calzones

1 large green bell pepper, coarsely chopped
½ (8-ounce package) sliced mushrooms
1 clove garlic, minced
¼ teaspoon Italian seasoning
1 (1 lb. 13-ounce) can reduced-fat refrigerated large buttermilk biscuits
2 cups chopped cooked chicken
1 cup shredded mozzarella cheese
Commercial spaghetti sauce

A calzone is like a turnover stuffed with pizza ingredients. Serving calzones with spaghetti or marinara sauce completes this Italian dish.

Preheat oven to 375°.

Place a nonstick skillet coated with vegetable cooking spray over medium-high heat; add pepper, mushrooms, garlic, and Italian seasoning. Cook 3 to 5 minutes, stirring occasionally, until peppers are tender.

Flatten each biscuit to a 6-inch circle using your hands or a rolling pin.

Place 4 flattened biscuits on a lightly greased baking sheet. Top each with ½ cup chicken, ¼ cup cheese, and one-fourth of the mushroom mixture. Top each with a remaining biscuit, pressing edges together with fork to seal.

Bake 11 to 13 minutes or until golden brown. Heat sauce, and serve with calzones.

Yield: 4 servings.

Note: You will need to use the extra large biscuits, such as Pillsbury's Grands, to make a 6-inch calzone. There's no need to flour your counter.

Broccoli-Ham Pockets with Honey Mustard Sauce

1 (10-ounce) package frozen chopped broccoli
1 (1 lb. 13-ounce) package reduced-fat refrigerated large buttermilk biscuits
1 cup shredded Cheddar or Swiss cheese
1 cup chopped cooked ham
Dried thyme
Honey-Mustard Sauce (page 72)

Preheat oven to 375°.

Cook broccoli according to package directions; drain well.

Flatten each biscuit to a 6-inch circle using your hands or a rolling pin.

Place 4 flattened biscuits on a lightly greased baking sheet. Top each with ¼ cup cheese, ¼ cup ham, ¼ cup broccoli, and a small pinch of thyme. (If broccoli pieces are large, chop to a finer consistency.)

Top each with a remaining biscuit, pressing edges together with fork to seal.

Bake 11 to 13 minutes or until golden brown. Heat Honey-Mustard Sauce and drizzle over pockets or use as a dipping sauce.

Yield: 4 servings.

Note: You will need to use the extra large biscuits, such as Pillsbury's Grands, to make a 6-inch calzone. There's no need to flour your counter.

Miss Ann's Tabbouleh Pitas

Tabbouleh may also be served as a side dish with grilled meats or sandwiches.

½ cup bulghur wheat or cracked wheat
2 large tomatoes, coarsely chopped
1 cucumber, peeled and chopped
1 bunch green onions, chopped
1 cup chopped fresh mint or parsley
⅓ cup fresh lemon juice
½ cup olive oil
1 tablespoon salt
½ teaspoon pepper
4 pita bread rounds
Lettuce

Rinse bulghur in hot water; drain well, squeezing excess water from bulghur.

Combine bulghur, tomatoes, cucumber, onions, mint, lemon juice, oil, salt, and pepper in a large bowl. Chill 1 hour or until bulghur absorbs liquid.

Slice pita bread in half, and separate to make pockets. Serve tabbouleh in pita bread lined with lettuce leaves.

Yield: 4 servings.

Note: This dish comes together by feel more than precise measuring. Make it once and adjust to your taste.

Don't be intimidated if you've never used bulghur wheat, also known as burghul; it's easy. In rural markets, your grocer may have to order it for you.

Chutney-Ham Croissants

Chutney gives this salad a tangy, spirited boost. Look for chutney in the condiment section of your supermarket.

1 (8-ounce) package Neufchâtel light cream cheese, softened
2 cups chopped cooked ham
½ cup commercial chutney
2 stalks celery, chopped
4 croissants
Lettuce

Combine cream cheese, ham, chutney, and celery, stirring well.

Spoon into croissants lined with lettuce.

Yield: 4 servings.

Breakfast Anytime

Life, within doors, has few pleasanter prospects than a neatly arranged and well-provisioned breakfast table.

Nathaniel Hawthorne

Conversation Starters

- **THESE RULES ARE MADE FOR BREAKIN'**
Jot down a few etiquette rules on index cards. Ask family members to select one at the table. During the meal, each person has to BREAK that rule. The person who catches the most "violations" wins the first piece of dessert that night.

- **SUPPER SAFARI**
Hunt down the answers to these questions at your next meal.

    1. If you could be any animal, what would you choose?

    2. What animal looks the funniest?

    3. What animal eats the weirdest things?

Country Sausage Quiche

1 green bell pepper, chopped
1 onion, thinly sliced
1 pound light turkey-and-pork ground
  sausage
2 unbaked 9-inch pie shells
2 cups shredded Cheddar cheese
5 large eggs
1 (5-ounce) can fat-free evaporated
  skimmed milk
1 (3-ounce) can sliced mushrooms,
  drained

This recipe from Susan's sister, Tamara Dosier-Vinay, makes two quick quiches for a crowd or an extra one to take to a neighbor.

Preheat oven to 350°.

Coat a large nonstick skillet with vegetable cooking spray and place over medium-high heat. Add pepper and onion; cook 3 minutes, stirring occasionally. Add sausage. Brown 3 to 5 minutes or until sausage is no longer pink, crumbling with a wooden spoon. (Reduce heat to medium if pan starts to get too hot.) Drain, if necessary.

Divide sausage mixture between two pie shells. Sprinkle evenly with cheese.

Whisk together eggs, evaporated milk, and mushrooms. Pour evenly into pie shells.

Bake 35 to 40 minutes or until golden.

Yield: 2 quiches; each quiche will serve 4 to 6.

Spinach-and-Mushroom Pie in Cheddar Crust

In fall or winter, serve this breakfast pie with hash browns and a citrus medley. In summer, pair it with chopped tomatoes with fresh basil and melon slices.

2 tablespoons butter
1 onion, chopped
1 (8-ounce) package sliced mushrooms
2 tablespoons all-purpose flour
1 cup half-and-half
1 (9-ounce) package frozen spinach, thawed and drained
1 teaspoon salt
1 teaspoon hot pepper sauce (optional)
3 large eggs, lightly beaten
Cheddar Cheese Pie Crust
½ cup shredded Cheddar cheese

Preheat oven to 375°.

Melt butter in a large saucepan over medium-high heat. Add onions and mushrooms; cook 3 to 4 minutes or until tender, stirring occasionally. Add flour, stirring to blend well. Cook 1 minute.

Add half-and-half, spinach, salt, and, if desired, pepper sauce; cook 2 minutes over medium heat. Remove from heat. Gradually stir about one-fourth of hot mixture into eggs; add to remaining hot mixture, stirring constantly.

Pour filling into cheese crust. Sprinkle with shredded cheese. Bake 35 minutes, shielding edges of pie with aluminum foil to avoid overbrowning, if necessary.

Yield: 8 servings.

Cheddar Cheese Pie Crust:
1 cup shredded Cheddar cheese
¾ cup all-purpose flour
½ teaspoon salt
¼ cup butter, melted

Combine cheese, flour, salt, and butter; press into bottom and sides of 9-inch deep-dish pie plate. Set aside.

Yield: 1 (9-inch) pie shell

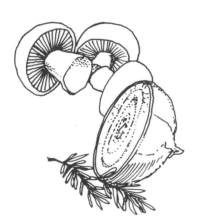

kid friendly

Dutch Baby Pancake with Fresh Berries

This recipe dresses up a simple pancake batter. Substitute whatever fresh fruit is in season.

1 cup strawberries, halved
1 cup fresh peach slices
1 cup fresh blueberries
½ cup sugar, divided
5 large eggs
1¼ cups milk
½ cup butter, melted
1 teaspoon vanilla extract
1¼ cups all-purpose flour
¼ teaspoon salt
Powdered sugar (optional)

Preheat oven to 425°.

Place a 12-inch cast-iron or oven-safe skillet in oven for 5 minutes or until hot.

Combine fruit and ¼ cup sugar in a large bowl, stirring occasionally until sugar melts; set aside.

Combine remaining ¼ cup sugar, eggs, milk, butter, vanilla, flour, and salt using a wire whisk to remove lumps. Pour into hot skillet.

Bake 20 minutes. (Pancake will rise and fall.) Spoon fruit into center; sprinkle with powdered sugar, if desired. Serve immediately.

Yield: 6 servings.

Note: Frozen fruit can be substituted, but let it thaw first. Spoon onto pancake with a slotted spoon.

Cinnamon-Oatmeal Griddle Cakes

1 cup milk
¾ cup quick-cooking oatmeal
3 tablespoons butter, melted
2 large eggs, lightly beaten
¾ cup all-purpose flour
2 teaspoons baking powder
¼ teaspoon salt
¼ cup firmly packed brown sugar
¼ teaspoon ground cinnamon

Heat milk in a small saucepan over medium heat (do not boil); remove from heat. Stir in oatmeal; let stand 10 minutes.

Stir in butter and eggs.

Combine flour, baking powder, salt, and sugar, and cinnamon in a large mixing bowl. Fold in oatmeal mixture. Gently stir in additional milk if batter is too thick.

Heat a lightly greased griddle or nonstick skillet over medium heat until hot. Pour ¼ cup batter onto skillet. Cook 1 to 2 minutes or until bubbles form on top of griddle cake. Flip and cook until done. Repeat with remaining batter. Serve with butter and maple syrup, if desired.

Yield: 4 servings.

Oatmeal packs extra nutrition and great flavor into these flapjacks.

Baked French Toast with Maple Praline Sauce

This make-ahead breakfast is perfect for serving a crowd. Baking, instead of pan-frying the French toast, lets you serve everyone at once—and it's never greasy.

½ (8-ounce) package cream cheese, softened
½ cup sifted powdered sugar
1 (16-ounce) loaf unsliced French bread
8 large eggs, lightly beaten
¾ cup half-and-half
1 teaspoon vanilla extract
¼ teaspoon ground cinnamon
Maple-Praline Sauce

Combine cream cheese and powdered sugar in a small bowl; set aside.

Cut bread into 1-inch slices to yield 20 pieces (don't use end pieces). Spread cream cheese mixture onto top of 10 pieces and top with remaining bread to resemble a sandwich.

Combine eggs, half-and-half, vanilla, and cinnamon in a 13- x 9-inch baking dish.

Add bread, turning several times to coat. Cover and refrigerate 8 hours or overnight.

Preheat oven to 375°. Remove bread from baking dish, discarding any excess liquid, and place on lightly greased baking sheet. Bake 20 to 25 minutes until golden brown. Serve with Maple-Praline Sauce.

Yield: 10 servings.

Maple-Praline Sauce:
½ cup butter
½ cup firmly packed light brown sugar
½ cup maple syrup
1 cup chopped pecans

Combine butter, sugar, syrup, and pecans in a small saucepan. Cook over medium-low heat, stirring often, until well blended.

Yield: 1¾ cups.

Note: Presliced French bread may be used but you'll have a few extra pieces. Cut into cubes for making salad croutons or stuffing and freeze until needed.

Rise 'n Shine Blueberry Bran Muffins

2 cups shredded bran cereal
1¼ cups skim milk
¼ cup applesauce
1 large egg
1¼ cup all-purpose flour
½ cup firmly packed brown sugar
4 teaspoons baking powder
¼ teaspoon salt
1 cup fresh or frozen blueberries
1 teaspoon vanilla extract
Buttery Bran-Streusel Topping (optional)

Preheat oven to 400°.

Combine cereal, milk, applesauce, and egg in a large bowl. Let stand 10 minutes.

Combine flour, sugar, baking powder, and salt. Add dry mixture to bran mixture, stirring gently to combine (do not over mix). Stir in blueberries and vanilla.

Spoon batter into a lightly greased 12-cup muffin pan. Sprinkle with topping, if desired.

Bake 20 minutes. Let stand in pans 1 minute; then remove.

Yield: 12 muffins.

Note: For testing we used All-Bran cereal. You can experiment with equal amounts of different fruits such as dried apricots, chopped apples, raisins, etc.

Per serving (without topping): 131 calories, 1.1 g. fat, 18 mg. cholesterol, 189 mg. sodium

Buttery Bran-Streusel Topping:
½ cup butter
2 tablespoons all-purpose flour
3 tablespoons light brown sugar
4 tablespoons shredded bran cereal

Combine flour, sugar, and cereal in a small bowl. Cut in butter with a fork or pastry blender until crumbly. Sprinkle over muffins and bake as directed.

Per serving (with topping): 221 calories, 8.7 g. fat, 39 mg. cholesterol, 280 mg. sodium

Blueberry-Lemon Bran Muffins:
Combine blueberries with 2 tablespoons fresh lemon juice and ½ teaspoon grated rind from 1 lemon. Proceed with recipe. Add ½ teaspoon grated lemon rind to topping.

We replaced the fat in this muffin with applesauce, so it's extra light. For a richer muffin, add the Buttery Bran-Streusel Topping.

Fluffy Cheese-and-Sausage Casserole

Try this great addition to your weekend breakfast line-up. You can prepare the casserole ahead and place, unbaked, in the refrigerator overnight. It may take a few extra minutes to bake once it's been chilled.

1 (12-ounce) package light turkey-and-pork sausage
3 tablespoons butter, softened
9 (1-inch-thick) slices French bread
2 cups shredded Cheddar cheese
6 large eggs, lightly beaten
3 cups milk
1 tablespoon Worcestershire sauce
½ teaspoon hot sauce

Brown sausage in a large nonstick skillet over medium-high heat, 3 to 5 minutes, or until meat is no longer pink, crumbling with a wooden spoon. Drain and set aside.

Spread butter on both sides of bread slices, and cut into 1-inch cubes. Place bread cubes in a lightly greased 13- x 9-inch baking dish. Sprinkle sausage and cheese evenly over bread.

Combine eggs, milk, Worcestershire, and pepper sauce. Pour over casserole.

Bake, covered, 45 minutes. Uncover and bake 5 minutes or until golden brown.

Yield: 6 to 8 servings.

Cranberry-Baked Apples

⅓-½ cup orange juice
8 Granny Smith apples, unpeeled
⅓ cup dried cranberries
½ cup firmly packed light brown sugar
¼ cup butter, cut into pieces
¼ cup chopped fresh mint leaves

Preheat oven to 375°.

Pour orange juice into lightly greased 13- x 9-inch baking dish.

Core apples and cut into wedges. Add to orange juice, tossing to coat. Add additional orange juice, if necessary. Stir in cranberries.

Sprinkle apple mixture with sugar and dot with butter.

Bake 20 to 30 minutes or until apples are tender and bubbly. Just before serving, stir in fresh mint.

Yield: 8 to 10 servings.

Note: 1 cup fresh or frozen cranberries may be substituted for dried cranberries (such as craisins). To make ahead, assemble dish as directed and refrigerate; bake it right before serving.

Baked apples are a Western North Carolina and East Tennessee tradition. Cranberries and mint make these extra special.

kid friendly

Quick Cheese Grits

Looking for a perfect brunch menu? Here's what Susan served for her daughter Frances's christening brunch: Quick Cheese Grits, spiral sliced ham, biscuits, her grandma's homemade jelly, and the Cranberry-Baked Apples (page 131). Scrumptious. And easy, too.

Grits are made from ground corn.
Polenta is the Italian food lover's version of grits. Both can be boiled or baked and served for breakfast, as an appetizer, or side dish.

6 cups water
½ teaspoon salt
1½ cups quick-cooking grits
½ cup half-and-half
3 cups shredded Cheddar cheese
½ teaspoon garlic powder
1-2 tablespoons Worcestershire sauce

Coat a heavy-duty pot or Dutch oven with vegetable cooking spray to make cleanup easier. Add water and salt; bring to a boil.

Stir in grits. Reduce heat to medium-low, and cook 5 to 7 minutes, stirring often.

Add half-and-half, cheese, garlic powder, and Worcestershire sauce. Cook 2 additional minutes, stirring well. Serve immediately.

Yield: 8 servings.

Note: To make ahead, prepare recipe as directed. Spoon into a lightly greased 2½-quart baking dish. Cover and refrigerate overnight. To reheat, bake at 350° for 50 minutes or until heated through.

Sides & Salads

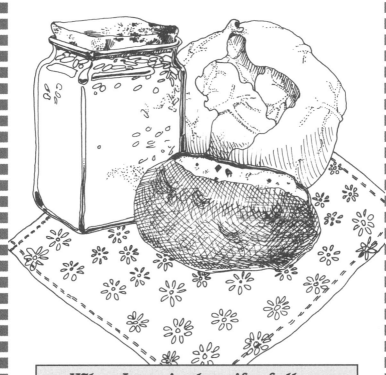

What I say is that, if a fellow really likes potatoes, he must be a decent sort of fellow.

A.A. Milne

Conversation Starters

- **SNOW BUNNIES**
Greet the first snow of the season with a snowball fight, followed by a hearty soup or stew.

- **FRONT AND CENTER**
Make place cards for family members or dinner guests by using inexpensive frames and baby pictures.

- **POTLUCK PANACHE**
Cooking a big batch? Invite your neighbors. Ask them to bring dessert or a big salad. Select a few fun questions in advance to get people talking. "Describe your first kiss" and "tell your most embarrassing moment" always works.

Honey-Roasted Carrots

1 pound baby carrots
¼ cup honey
1 teaspoon salt-free seasoning blend
¼ cup butter, cut into pieces

Preheat oven to 400°.

Place carrots into a lightly greased 11- x 7-inch baking dish. Drizzle with honey, and sprinkle with seasoning blend. Top with butter pieces.

Bake 45 to 50 minutes or until carrots are tender.

Yield: 4 servings.

Note: We used Mrs. Dash original seasoning for salt-free blend. Lemon-pepper blend can be substituted.

This mouthwatering recipe from Beryl Flurry perks up any menu. For variety, she sometimes mixes the carrots with new potatoes.

Corn Pudding

1 (1-pound) bag frozen corn, thawed and drained
5 large eggs, lightly beaten
1½ cups milk
¼ cup butter, melted
¼ cup onion, chopped
2 teaspoons sugar (optional)
1 teaspoon salt
1 teaspoon pepper

Preheat oven to 350°.

Combine all ingredients. Place in a lightly greased 11-x 7-inch casserole dish. Bake for 1 hour, uncovered, or until knife inserted in center comes out clean.

Yield: 6 to 8 servings.

Down South, we like a little sugar in our corn pudding, but the choice is yours!

kid friendly

Angel's Rice

¼ cup butter

1 angel hair pasta nest, broken into fourths (enough for 1 cup) or 1 cup broken vermicelli or spaghetti noodles

2 cups converted rice

3¾ cups chicken broth

½ teaspoon salt

Melt butter in a large skillet over medium heat. Add angel hair pasta and cook, stirring constantly, until pasta is light brown and mixture sizzles.

Add rice, broth, and salt. Bring to boil over medium-high heat. Cover and reduce heat to medium-low. Simmer 15 to 20 minutes until water is absorbed and rice is tender.

Yield: 8 servings.

This recipe comes from Ann Bajalia, a Jerusalem-born American and a fabulous cook. Even very young children love this dish.

Broccoli-Pecan Casserole

1 (1-pound) package frozen broccoli
1 (10¾-ounce) can condensed cream of roasted garlic and mushroom soup
¼ cup mayonnaise
¼ cup sour cream
½ cup chopped pecans
½ cup Cheddar-Crunch Topping

Preheat oven to 350°.

Cook broccoli according to package directions; drain. Combine broccoli, soup, mayonnaise, sour cream, and nuts.

Pour broccoli mixture into lightly greased 9-inch square baking dish.

Sprinkle Cheddar-Crunch Topping over casserole. Bake for 20 minutes.

Yield: 4 to 6 servings.

Cheddar-Crunch Topping:
¼ cup butter, softened
¼ cup shredded Cheddar cheese
8 saltine crackers, finely crushed

Combine ingredients.

Yield: ½ cup.

Double the Cheddar topping, and freeze half to use on other casseroles or vegetables.

Cauliflower Au Gratin

Try this recipe before you decide you don't like cauliflower—it has earned more than a few converts. If you're still not convinced, try the broccoli variation.

1 large head cauliflower, cut into florets
½ cup mayonnaise
1 tablespoon hot Chinese or Dijon
    mustard
1 cup shredded Swiss cheese
2 tablespoons seasoned dry
    breadcrumbs

Preheat oven to 400°.

Boil cauliflower 5 minutes or until tender; drain. Place cauliflower in lightly greased 9-inch square baking dish.

Combine mayonnaise and mustard. Spread mixture over cauliflower and sprinkle with cheese and breadcrumbs.

Bake 10 to 15 minutes until lightly browned and bubbly.

Yield: 4 to 6 servings.

Chinese hot mustard will give this dish a bit of heat. If you like spicy foods, increase mustard to 2 tablespoons.

Broccoli Au Gratin:

Substitute 1 head broccoli florets for cauliflower.

Cauliflower's pretty white florets must be shielded from the sun when grown; otherwise, the natural chlorophyll in the plant will turn its head green.

Maple Roasted Sweet Potatoes

Julia combined these five ingredients to put a new, quick twist on classic sweet potatoes.

3 large sweet potatoes (about 3 pounds), peeled and cubed
1 (12-ounce) package fresh or frozen cranberries
½ cup butter, melted
½ cup maple syrup
½ cup chopped pecans, toasted

Preheat oven to 375°.

Place sweet potatoes and cranberries in a large, lightly greased roasting pan.

Combine butter and maple syrup. Pour over sweet potatoes and cranberries, stirring to coat. Cover tightly with foil.

Bake 20 to 25 minutes or until potatoes are tender. Spoon into serving dish and sprinkle with pecans.

Yield: 6 to 8 servings.

Real maple syrup is the boiled down sap of a maple tree. Maple syrup became popular with Early American colonists because of the high cost of sugar. Nowadays, it's the real maple syrup that's more expensive than sugar.

Mashed Sweet Potatoes for a Crowd

Irish potatoes aren't the only kind that taste splendid when mashed, especially when spiced with ginger and cinnamon.

5 large sweet potatoes
½-¾ cup chicken broth
¼ cup butter
½ cup low-fat sour cream
¾ teaspoon ground ginger
½ teaspoon ground cinnamon
Salt to taste

Peel sweet potatoes; place in a large bowl. Add ½ cup water. Loosely cover with plastic wrap. Microwave at HIGH 10 minutes; rotate bowl quarter-turn. Microwave at HIGH 10 minutes. Check potatoes for doneness. (Be careful not to let escaping steam burn you.) You should be able to gently prick the potatoes with a fork with little resistance. Microwave at HIGH an additional 2 minutes until potatoes are tender, if needed.

Drain potatoes and mash with a fork or electric mixer on medium speed. Add ½ cup chicken broth, butter, sour cream, ginger, cinnamon, and salt. If you desire a thinner mashed potato, add the remaining ¼ cup broth.

Yield: 10 servings.

Note: If you're making this ahead, simply cover and reheat in the microwave for 12 to 15 minutes before serving.

Nutty, Crispy Green Beans

2 tablespoons butter
2 tablespoons olive oil
1½ pounds fresh green beans, trimmed
2-3 cloves garlic, minced
½ cup chopped walnuts
1 teaspoon salt
½ teaspoon pepper
¼ cup freshly grated Parmesan cheese
   (optional)

Heat butter and oil in large nonstick skillet; add beans, garlic, and walnuts. Cook 10 to 12 minutes over medium heat, stirring often until crisp-tender. Cover and let stand 5 minutes.

Stir in salt and pepper; sprinkle with cheese, if desired.

Yield: 6 servings.

Note: If you prefer a less crispy bean, steam or boil beans 5 minutes before adding to recipe.

Try this conversation starter: One family member starts a story with a few sentences. The story is completed as dinner participants each add their sentences to the tale.

Snappy Baked Tomatoes

3 medium tomatoes
¼ cup fat-free Ranch salad dressing
¼ cup shredded mozzarella cheese
2 tablespoons seasoned dry
      breadcrumbs

Preheat oven to 450°.

Slice tomatoes in half; scoop out and discard seeds. Spoon dressing into tomato halves.

Combine cheese and breadcrumbs. Top tomato halves with cheese mixture. Place on a lightly greased baking sheet.

Bake tomatoes 12 inches from heat for 5 to 8 minutes until cheese is bubbly and browned.

Yield: 3 to 6 servings.

Per serving: 51 calories, 1.3 g. fat, 4 mg. cholesterol, 191 mg. sodium

Technically a fruit, the government classified the tomato as a vegetable for trade purposes, and it has been considered so for over 100 years. Do you know why tomatoes are really a fruit?

Carolina Cole Slaw

½ cup sugar
½ cup white vinegar
½ cup ketchup
¼ cup vegetable oil
¼ teaspoon salt
¼ teaspoon garlic powder
½ large head cabbage, shredded
1 green bell pepper, coarsely chopped

Combine sugar, vinegar, ketchup, oil, salt, and garlic powder in a large glass measuring cup. Cover and microwave at HIGH 2½ minutes.

Combine cabbage and green pepper in a large bowl. Pour hot mixture over vegetables. Chill at least two hours.

Yield: 8 to 10 servings.

Note: One (16-ounce) bag cole slaw mix may be substituted for the cabbage and green pepper.

This tangy, vinegar-based cole slaw is traditionally paired with Lexington, North Carolina-style barbecue, but you can enjoy it with most any dish.

Classic Apple-Spinach Salad

Don't worry about the chopped apples turning brown if you are making this recipe ahead of time. Just stir them into the salad dressing, and the vinegar will keep the apples bright.

½ cup apple cider vinegar
½ cup sugar
¼ cup vegetable oil
½ teaspoon salt
¼ teaspoon dry mustard
1 (10-ounce) bag fresh spinach, stems removed, if desired
1 tart, red apple, cored and chopped
½ red onion, quartered and thinly sliced (optional)
½ cup toasted pecans

Combine vinegar, sugar, oil, salt, and dry mustard in a large jar or container with lid. Shake vigorously.

Toss spinach, apples, and, if desired, onion with salad dressing in a large bowl. Sprinkle with toasted pecans.

Yield: 4 to 6 servings.

Appalachian Spinach Salad:
Add ½ cup of slivered, cooked country ham when you add pecans.

Herb-Marinated Shrimp Salad

2 pounds medium-size fresh shrimp
1 sweet onion, quartered and sliced
1 red bell pepper, diced
⅓ cup light olive oil
¼ cup fresh lemon juice
¼ cup rice or white wine vinegar
1 clove garlic, minced
2 tablespoons chopped fresh basil
1 tablespoon chopped fresh parsley
1 tablespoon chopped fresh chives
1 teaspoon chopped fresh thyme
1 teaspoon sugar
1 teaspoon salt
1 teaspoon freshly ground pepper

Bring 6 cups water to a boil in a large pot. Add shrimp and cook 3 to 5 minutes or until shrimp turn pink. Drain and rinse with cold water.

Peel and devein shrimp.

Combine shrimp and remaining ingredients. Cover and chill until serving.

Yield: 4 main dish or 6 side dish servings.

Note: Try Vidalia, Walla-Walla, Texas Sweet, or any other sweet spring onion in this recipe. If you use a regular "hot" onion, you may want to use only half to keep from overpowering the fresh herbs.

Julia has made this recipe for cooking demonstrations and parties. The fresh herbs ignite the tastebuds. To make this fabulous dish super-quick, buy shrimp already steamed at the seafood counter.

Steak-Lover's Salad with Fresh Tomato Vinaigrette

By using Roma tomatoes and broiling (rather than grilling) the beef, you can enjoy this summer-fresh salad any time of the year. Not in the mood for a salad? Simply serve crusty bread with the beef, and spoon the Fresh Tomato Vinaigrette over the meat as if it were a salsa.

1 (10-ounce) bag mixed salad greens
Italian Broiled Steak, thinly sliced
   (page 65)
Fresh Tomato Vinaigrette

Arrange greens on 4 serving plates. Fan slices of steak over greens. Serve with desired amount of Fresh Tomato Vinaigrette.

Yield: 4 servings.

Fresh Tomato Vinaigrette:
¼ cup red wine vinegar
3 tablespoons olive oil
1 tablespoon water
1 teaspoon sugar
½ teaspoon Dijon mustard
¼ teaspoon salt
¼ teaspoon garlic powder
2 large Roma tomatoes, chopped
1 tablespoon chopped fresh basil or
   oregano

Combine vinegar, oil, water, sugar, mustard, salt, and garlic powder in a large container with lid; shake vigorously. Stir in fresh tomatoes and herbs. Let stand 10 minutes. Stir well before serving.

Yield: 1½ cups.

Sweet Marinated Veggie Salad

kid friendly

1 cup chopped celery
1 large green bell pepper, seeded and chopped
1 onion, chopped
1 (15-ounce) can baby green peas, drained
1 (14.5-ounce) can no-salt French-style green beans, drained
1 (11-ounce) can white shoepeg corn, drained
1 (2-ounce) jar sliced pimientos, drained
Sweet Marinade

Stir together celery, pepper, onion, peas, green beans, corn, and pimientos. Pour Sweet Marinade over vegetables, and stir well. Let stand at least 1 hour. Serve cold or at room temperature.

Yield: 6 to 8 servings.

Sweet Marinade:
½ cup sugar
½ cup white wine vinegar
¼ cup vegetable oil
½ teaspoon salt
½ teaspoon pepper

Combine all ingredients in a large glass cup or bowl. Microwave at HIGH 2 minutes or until mixture boils.

Yield: 1 cup.

Fancy Marinated Veggie Salad:
Substitute brown sugar for white sugar, and add 1(3-ounce) jar capers and ½ cup sliced ripe olives.

This easy recipe from our friend Ruthann Betz-Essinger is perfect for a quick side dish, picnics, and family reunions. It can be made the day ahead and will even keep up to one week in the refrigerator.

Wagon Wheel Pasta Salad

Experiment with adding your favorite fresh vegetables to this basic salad. For a heartier salad, add chopped roast beef or chicken.

8 ounces wagon wheel pasta, uncooked
1 cup reduced-calorie Caesar or Ranch salad dressing
½ cup light mayonnaise
1 head fresh broccoli, cut into florets
1 red bell pepper, seeded and coarsely chopped
¼ cup freshly grated Parmesan cheese

Cook pasta according to package directions; rinse in cold water, and drain.

Combine dressing and mayonnaise in a large bowl. Stir in broccoli, pepper, and cheese. Chill 4 at least hours before serving.

Yield: 8 to 10 servings.

Desserts

Once in a young lifetime
one should be allowed to have as
much sweetness as one
can possibly want to hold.

Judith Olney

Conversation Starters

- **LEFT IS RIGHT, AND RIGHT IS LEFT**
Eat dinner with the other hand.

- **LET'S JAM...OR JUST RELAX**
Each night, let one member of the family select music to accompany dinner. (Volume is still up to the parents.)

- **BAY AT THE MOON**
Texan Liz Carpenter, former press secretary for Lady Bird Johnson, loves to talk about her "Bay at the Moon" gatherings where she and her most spirited friends literally howl at a full moon. You can host one, too. A quick look at the encyclopedia under "Moon" provides further discussion over dinner or a midnight snack.

Peanut Butter-Banana Bread

Applesauce replaces the oil in this recipe for a lower-fat, high-flavor bread.

1½ cups all-purpose flour
½ cup sugar
¾ teaspoon baking soda
½ teaspoon salt
2 very ripe bananas
2 large eggs
¼ cup applesauce
¾ cup creamy peanut butter
½ cup chopped peanuts

Preheat oven to 350°.

Combine flour, sugar, baking soda, and salt in a large bowl.

Mash bananas with a fork; stir in eggs, applesauce, peanut butter, and peanuts. Add banana mixture to flour mixture and stir until blended.

Pour mixture into a lightly greased 9- x 5- x 3-inch loaf pan, and bake 45 minutes or until loaf is golden brown and a toothpick inserted into the center comes out clean.

Yield: 15 servings.

Note: If you're out of applesauce and have vegetable oil on hand, you may substitute it in equal amounts for the applesauce; you may also use crunchy peanut butter and omit the peanuts. Reduced-fat peanut butter works in this recipe, too.

Per serving: 202 calories, 9.7 g. fat, 29 mg. cholesterol, 206 mg. sodium

Peanut Butter-Chocolate Chip Banana Bread:
Substitute ½ cup semisweet chocolate morsels for the chopped peanuts.

Peanuts aren't nuts; they're actually legumes. (A bean is a legume.) Peanut plants flower above ground, then bend to the soil to bury the pods. Almost half of all peanuts grown will be made into peanut butter.

White Chocolate Bread Pudding

Bread pudding is such a delicious dessert, it 's hard to believe it's a "left-over" made from stale bread.

1 (16-ounce) loaf stale French bread, cut into 1-inch cubes
1 cup white chocolate morsels
4 cups (1 quart) milk
¼ cup butter
1 cup sugar
5 eggs, lightly beaten
¼ teaspoon salt
1 teaspoon vanilla extract
½ teaspoon cinnamon
Best Ever Caramel Sauce (page 166)

Preheat oven to 375°.

Place bread cubes in a lightly greased 13- x 9-inch baking dish. Sprinkle with morsels.

Heat milk and butter until hot in a medium saucepan. Add sugar, stirring until melted.

Slowly pour 1 cup hot milk mixture into eggs, stirring constantly.

Pour egg mixture into remaining milk mixture. Stir in salt, vanilla, and cinnamon.

Pour mixture over bread and morsels. Bake for 45 minutes. Mixture will be soft, but should hold its shape when served. Serve warm with caramel sauce.

Yield: 10 to 12 servings.

Chocolate-Raspberry Oatmeal Bars

1 cup all-purpose flour
2 cups regular or quick oats
½ cup sugar
½ cup firmly packed brown sugar
1 teaspoon baking powder
1 cup butter
1 (10-ounce) jar seedless raspberry
    preserves
1 cup semisweet chocolate morsels

Preheat oven to 375°.

Combine flour, oats, sugars, and baking powder.

Cut in butter with a pastry blender or fork until crumbly; set aside 1½ cups. Press remaining flour mixture into bottom of an ungreased 13- x 9-inch baking pan. Bake 10 minutes.

Spread preserves over crust; sprinkle evenly with morsels. Sprinkle reserved flour mixture over morsels. Bake for 30 minutes or until golden brown. Cool; cut into 1- x 3-inch bars.

Yield: 3 dozen.

Raspberry bars have been a favorite for kids and adults for years. Julia couldn't resist combining two of her favorite flavors—raspberry and chocolate. These bars are dainty enough for showers and teas, yet filling enough for an everyday snack.

Chocolate-Strawberry Trifle

This easy dessert serves a small crowd, and it's a great way to use leftover angel food cake.

3 cups fresh sliced strawberries
½ cup sugar
1 teaspoon vanilla extract
1 (8-ounce) carton light sour cream
1 (8-ounce) carton light frozen whipped topping, thawed
½ of a (10-inch) angel food cake
Chocolate Mint Sauce

Combine berries, sugar, and vanilla in a bowl. Stir well and set aside.

Fold together sour cream and whipped topping. Tear angel food cake into 1-inch pieces. Place half of cake pieces in bottom of a large glass trifle bowl or deep serving bowl; top with half of chocolate sauce, half of berries, and half of sour cream mixture. Repeat procedure again, ending with the sour cream mixture on top. Cover and chill at least 3 hours.

Yield: 10 servings.

Chocolate Mint Sauce:
¾ cup milk
1 (10-ounce) package mint chocolate morsels
1½ cups marshmallow creme

Heat milk in a heavy saucepan over medium heat. Stir in chocolate morsels and marshmallow creme. Cook, stirring constantly, until chocolate melts (do not let boil).

Yield: 1½ cups.

Note: For a lower-fat dessert, substitute 1 (3.4-ounce) package prepared fat-free instant chocolate pudding for the Chocolate Mint Sauce.

Per serving: 411 calories, 15.4 g. fat, 4 mg. cholesterol, 185 mg. sodium

Toasted Pecan Clusters

3 tablespoons butter
3 cups pecan halves
12 ounces sweet dark chocolate, chopped

Melt butter in a large skillet; add pecan halves and cook 5 minutes, stirring constantly, until toasted. (You should be able to smell the toasted pecans.) Let cool.

Heat chocolate over a double boiler, stirring frequently until melted (do not get too hot). Stir in pecans, tossing to coat.

Spoon 2 or 3 coated pecan halves on waxed paper to form cluster. Repeat with remaining pecan halves. Let set. Store in airtight container in a cool place.

Yield: about 5 dozen.

Note: Chocolate or vanilla almond bark can also be used.

It's hard to resist this easy-to-make candy. You can substitute your favorite semisweet, milk, or white chocolate.

kid friendly

Quick Strawberry Shortcake

You can use almost any frozen biscuit available in your market for this recipe.

1 quart fresh strawberries, halved
½ cup sugar
2 tablespoons butter, melted
2 tablespoons light brown sugar
8 frozen biscuits, halved
1 cup heavy whipping cream
2 tablespoons sugar

Combine berries and sugar in a large bowl; let stand 15 to 30 minutes.

Combine butter and brown sugar; brush over tops and insides of biscuits. Bake biscuits according to package directions.

Beat whipping cream at high speed with an electric mixer, gradually adding 2 tablespoons sugar, beating until soft peaks form; chill until serving.

Place one half of biscuit on a serving plate. Spoon a small amount of berries and whipped cream over biscuit; top with other half of biscuit. Spoon berries on top of biscuit and dollop with whipped cream. Repeat with remaining biscuits.

Yield: 8 servings.

Cranberry-Cream Cheese Pound Cake

kid friendly

1 cup dried cranberries
1 tablespoon all-purpose flour
1 cup butter, softened
1 (8-ounce) package cream cheese, softened
3 cups sugar
5 large eggs
3 cups all-purpose flour
½ cup milk
2 teaspoons vanilla extract

Preheat oven to 325°.

Toss cranberries with 1 tablespoon flour; set aside.

Beat butter and cream cheese at medium speed with an electric mixer 1 to 2 minutes. Add sugar, and beat 1 to 2 minutes.

Add eggs at once, and beat just until dark yellow yolk disappears into batter.

Take turns adding flour and milk to batter, blending after each addition. Stir in cranberries and vanilla.

Pour into a greased and floured 10-inch tube pan or 8-cup Bundt pan. Bake 1½ hours or until a wooden pick inserted near the center comes out clean. (The cracks in the top will look moist but not wet.) Cool 10 minutes. Remove from pan and let cool on wire rack.

Yield: one (10-inch) cake

If you use a regional brand of soft wheat flour such as White Lily or Martha White, decrease the milk in this recipe to ¼ cup. National brands, such as Pillsbury and Gold Medal, need ½ cup milk. We used Craisins for the dried cranberries.

Chocolate Pound Cake with Chocolate Chip Glaze

To soften butter or cream cheese, unwrap and microwave at HIGH 20 to 30 seconds.

Avoid using a low-calorie or whipped butter—the texture and flavor needs the higher-fat sticks. This mixing procedure is a little different from what you may be used to, but it's quicker, easier, and works beautifully.

1 cup butter, softened
½ cup vegetable shortening
2 cups sugar
1 cup firmly packed brown sugar
5 large eggs
2¾ cups all-purpose flour
¼ cup plus 1 tablespoon cocoa
½ teaspoon salt
1 cup milk
1 teaspoon vanilla extract
Chocolate Chip Glaze

Preheat oven to 325°.

Beat butter and shortening at medium speed of an electric mixer 1 to 2 minutes. Add sugars at once, and beat 1 to 2 minutes. Add eggs at once, and beat just until dark yellow yolk disappears into batter.

Combine flour, cocoa, and salt. Take turns adding flour mixture and milk to the batter, blending after each addition. Stir in vanilla.

Pour batter into a greased and floured 10-inch tube pan or 8-cup Bundt pan. Bake 1 hour and 10 minutes or until a wooden pick inserted near the center comes out clean. (The cracks in the top should look moist, but not wet.) Cool 10 minutes. Remove from pan and let cool on wire rack. Serve with Chocolate Chip Glaze.

Yield: 1 (10-inch) cake

Chocolate Chip Glaze:

**1 cup (6 ounces) semisweet chocolate
    morsels**
½ cup heavy whipping cream

Combine morsels and cream in a heavy saucepan over medium-low heat, stirring constantly until melted. Pour over cooled cake.

Yield: 1 cup.

Note: This glaze will not harden and will be slightly sticky to touch even after it's set on the cake. If desired, glaze may be stored in an airtight container and refrigerated. Reheat and serve warm over ice cream and cake.

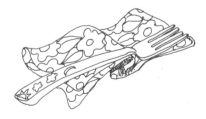

Graham-y Apple Crunch

Baking apples sit on round, smooth bottoms, unlike a Red Delicious (a beloved eating apple) that has a lumpy bottom.

2 tablespoons sugar
6 Granny Smith or other baking apples
6 cinnamon-graham crackers, crushed (about 1 cup)
½ cup firmly packed brown sugar
¼ cup all-purpose flour
¼ cup butter, cut into pieces

Preheat oven to 350°.

Peel and core apples. Slice thinly, and toss with sugar; set aside.

Combine cracker crumbs, brown sugar, and flour in a medium bowl. Cut in butter with a pastry blender or fork until crumbly; set aside.

Place apple slices in a lightly greased 8-inch square baking dish. Sprinkle evenly with crumb topping.

Bake 30 minutes or until golden brown and bubbly. Serve with ice cream, if desired.

Yield: 6 servings.

Per serving: 219 calories, 1.4 g. fat, 1 mg. cholesterol, 57 mg. sodium

Cinnamon-Chip Biscotti

The coffeehouse phenomenon made this crunchy Italian "dunking" cookie famous. For a great gift, give a batch along with coffee beans and a mug.

½ cup butter, softened
⅔ cup firmly packed light brown sugar
⅔ cup sugar
2 large eggs
2½ cups all-purpose flour
2 teaspoons baking powder
¼ teaspoon salt
½ teaspoon ground cinnamon
1 cup chopped pecans
1 cup semisweet chocolate mini-morsels

Preheat oven to 350°.

Combine butter and sugars in a large mixing bowl; beat at medium speed with an electric mixer until creamy. Add eggs, one at a time, beating until blended.

Combine flour, baking powder, salt, and cinnamon; add to butter mixture, beat at medium speed until blended. Fold in nuts and morsels.

Divide dough in half; shape each into a 12- x 2-inch log on a lightly greased baking sheet.

Bake for 20 minutes or until firm. Let cool on baking sheet 5 minutes. Transfer to wire racks to cool completely.

Cut each log into ½-inch-wide diagonal slices using a serrated knife. Place slices on ungreased baking sheets.

Bake for 7 minutes; turn over and bake another 7 minutes. Cool on wire racks.

Yield: 3 dozen.

Can you guess where cinnamon sticks come from? The pungent spice is the inner bark from a tropical evergreen tree that has dried and curled into sticks.

Wedding Cookies

These cookies are actually Mexican in origin. With these simple ingredients, you can enjoy them any day—not just wedding days.

1 cup butter, softened
¼ cup sifted powdered sugar
2 teaspoons vanilla extract
2 cups all-purpose flour
⅛ teaspoon salt
½ cup chopped pecans
Powdered sugar

Preheat oven to 325°.

Beat butter and sugar at medium speed of an electric mixer; stir in vanilla. Combine flour, salt, and nuts. Stir into butter mixture.

Roll dough into 1-inch balls. Place on baking sheet, and bake for 15 minutes. (The tops of the cookies will remain pale, and the bottoms will be a light golden brown.) Cool.

Roll cookies in powdered sugar to coat. Store in airtight container.

Yield: 3 dozen.

Almond Joyful Pie

kid friendly

⅔ cup sliced almonds
1 cup butter, melted
1 cup coconut
1 cup sugar
½ cup cocoa
¼ cup light corn syrup
3 large eggs, lightly beaten
1 teaspoon vanilla extract
⅛ teaspoon salt
1 unbaked 9-inch pastry shell

Preheat oven to 375°.

Sprinkle almonds on ungreased baking sheet; bake 3 to 5 minutes or until lightly browned; set aside.

Combine butter, coconut, sugar, cocoa, corn syrup, eggs, vanilla, salt, and almonds. Pour into pastry shell.

Bake 35 minutes or until set.

Yield: 1 (9-inch) pie

This terrific choco-late pie was inspired by one of our favorite candy bars.

kid friendly

Lemon-Buttermilk Custard Pie

This traditional custard pie is destined to become a family favorite.

½ (15-ounce) package refrigerated pie
  crusts
1 cup sugar
3 tablespoons all-purpose flour
3 large eggs
⅓ cup butter, melted
1 cup buttermilk
2 teaspoons grated lemon rind
2 tablespoons lemon juice
Sweetened whipped cream

Preheat oven to 375°.

Prepare pie crust according to package directions; do not bake.

Combine sugar and flour. Stir in eggs, butter, buttermilk, rind, and juice. Pour into prepared pie crust.

Bake 50 minutes, shielding edges with foil to prevent overbrowning, if necessary, until golden brown.(Pie will set more firmly as it cools.)

Yield: 1 (9-inch) pie.

Note: We love the flavor, texture and ease of refrigerated pie crusts but you can prepare a homemade crust or use a frozen one, too.

Peanut Butter Pie

1⅓ cups whipping cream, divided
1 (8-ounce) package cream cheese,
   softened
½ cup creamy peanut butter
½ cup powdered sugar
1 teaspoon vanilla extract
1 (9-inch) prepared chocolate-flavored
   pie crust
⅓ cup whipping cream
4 ounces semi-sweet chocolate, finely
   chopped
Garnish: whipped cream, chopped
   peanut butter cups

Beat 1 cup whipping cream at medium speed with electric mixer until soft peaks form (this should make about 2 cups whipped cream); set aside.

Combine cream cheese, peanut butter, sugar, and vanilla, beating until creamy.

Fold in whipped cream. Spoon into prepared pie crust. Freeze pie.

Heat remaining ⅓ cup whipping cream in microwave at HIGH for 30 seconds or until. Stir in chopped chocolate until melted. Microwave additional 15 seconds, if necessary.

Pour chocolate mixture over pie, and return to freezer. Freeze 2 to 3 hours until firm. Garnish with whipped cream and chopped peanut butter cups, if desired.

Yield: 1 (9-inch) pie

Occasionally you deserve to splurge. This rich dessert is worth every calorie. We insist that you try it!

The Best Ever Caramel Sauce

■ ■ ■ ■ ■ ■ ■ ■ ■ ■

Ice cream or angel food cake simply provide excuses to devour more divine sauce. We dare you not to lick the spoon!

½ cup butter
1 cup firmly packed light brown sugar
½ cup whipping cream
1 tablespoon vanilla extract

Combine butter and brown sugar in a heavy saucepan. Cook over medium heat, stirring often, until sugar melts.

Stir in whipping cream; bring mixture to a full boil and remove from heat. Stir in vanilla.

Yield: 1¼ cups.

Good Stuff

Almost every person has
something secret he likes to eat.

M.F.K. Fisher

Conversation Starters

- **HELPING HANDS**
Work together to make a dish to take to a homeless shelter or community center. A quick call before hand will help with logistics and recipe selection.

- **HARVEST HOME**
Take the kids or a gang of friends to the farmers market, a you-pick-it fruit farm, or roadside produce stand each season of the year. Then make a "Welcome the Season" dessert with your harvest.

- **TAKING A HIKE**
Forget cooking tonight. Call some friends and pick up take-out fried chicken. Truck to the closest state park or recreation area and take a hike. Designate someone to bring along a good ghost story to accompany dessert.

Garlic Monkey Bread

¼ cup butter, melted
¼ cup freshly grated Parmesan cheese
¼ teaspoon garlic powder
¼ cup chopped fresh parsley
2 (10.8-ounce) cans reduced-fat
   buttermilk biscuits

Preheat oven to 375°.

Combine butter, cheese, garlic powder, and parsley in large bowl.

Cut biscuits into quarters; dip into butter mixture, and layer in an 8-cup Bundt pan.

Bake 20 to 25 minutes until golden brown, covering with foil, if necessary, to prevent overbrowning.

Yield: 10 servings.

This easy pull-apart bread dresses up a vegetable plate or pasta meal.

Sour Cream-Cheddar Biscuits

So simple, so good! Serve this drop biscuit with soups, or whenever you want hot bread.

½ cup butter, melted
½ cup light sour cream
½ cup shredded Cheddar cheese
1 cup self-rising flour

Preheat oven to 400°.

Combine butter, sour cream, and cheese; stir in flour.

Drop batter by rounded teaspoonfuls into ungreased mini-muffin pan.

Bake 15 minutes or until lightly golden brown. Remove from pan immediately.

Yield: 2 dozen.

Note: If you do not have a mini-muffin pan, you can drop batter by teaspoonfuls onto an ungreased baking sheet.

Sweet Potato Rolls

 kid friendly

2 (29-ounce) cans yams (cut in syrup), drained
3 (¼-ounce) packages yeast
¾ cup warm (105° to 115°) water
7½ cups all-purpose flour
1 tablespoon baking powder
1 tablespoon salt
1½ cups butter, cut into pieces

Mash potatoes by hand or beat with an electric mixer until smooth.

Combine yeast and water in a small bowl; let stand 5 minutes.

Combine flour, baking powder, and salt in a large bowl. Cut in butter with a fork or pastry blender until mixture is crumbly.

Stir yeast mixture and sweet potatoes into flour mixture. (You may have to use your hands.) Turn dough out onto a lightly floured surface; knead 5 minutes. Place dough in a lightly greased bowl, turning to coat top of dough. Cover and refrigerate 8 hours or overnight.

Roll dough to ¾-inch thickness on a lightly floured surface, and cut with 2-inch round cutter. Place rolls on ungreased baking sheets; let rise in a warm place 20 minutes or until doubled in bulk.

Preheat oven to 400°. Bake 10 to 12 minutes until lightly browned.

Yield: 5 dozen.

Note: To freeze, bake rolls at 400° for 8 to 10 minutes; do not let rolls brown. Freeze in an airtight container or freezer bag up to 6 weeks. To serve, thaw and bake at 400° until browned.

Looking for a warm place for rolls to rise? If you have a double oven, you can place a small pan of boiling water in the bottom of one of the ovens. That will provide just the right amount of heat and humidity. Use the other oven for baking. If you're in a pinch, place a pan of rolls on a dryer that's just been turned off, or on the seat of a warm car.

Blue Cheese Bruschetta

In Italian, the word bruschetta means "to roast over coals" or in our American slang, toast. This simple recipe takes garlic bread to new heights. Paired with a salad, it's a meal.

½ (16-ounce) loaf French bread
Olive oil
1 tomato, cut into cubes
1-2 cloves garlic, minced
1 tablespoon fresh oregano
4 ounces crumbled blue cheese
¼ teaspoon salt
¼ teaspoon pepper

Cut French bread down the center, lengthwise, to make two long, skinny bases of bread. Cut into smaller pieces, if desired.

Grill or broil bread, turning once, until golden brown, about 3 minutes on each side; remove from heat and drizzle or brush cut side with olive oil

While bread toasts, toss together tomato, garlic, oregano, blue cheese, salt, and pepper, Spoon cheese mixture onto cut sides of bread, and serve immediately. If you want a creamier cheese texture, slide the bread back under the broiler for about 1 minute.

Yield: 2 sandwich servings or 6 to 8 snack servings.

Note: Blue cheese isn't on most kid's top ten list of foods. To make this recipe more kid-friendly, simply substitute shredded mozzarella cheese. You can also substitute ½ teaspoon dried oregano for fresh.

Almost Fresh Salsa

When tomatoes are not in season, use canned, diced tomatoes. They give you the color, taste and juice needed for this great salsa.

1   (14.5-ounce) can diced tomatoes
1   jalapeño pepper, chopped
1   clove garlic, chopped
¼   cup chopped red onion
2   tablespoons chopped fresh cilantro
2   tablespoons lime juice
¼   teaspoon salt

Combine ingredients; cover and chill until serving.

Yield: 2 cups.

Per (2 tablespoon) serving: 8 calories, 0.1 g. fat, 0 mg. cholesterol, 88 mg. sodium

Like snowflakes, no two jalapeño peppers are alike; some are hotter than others. The punch in the peppers comes from the seeds and ribs—remove them (using gloves if necessary) for milder dishes.

Bandit's Salsa

Black beans and corn make a colorful addition to a traditional salsa recipe. It's easy when you start with a jar of salsa. The flavor gets even better after standing a few hours.

1   (16-ounce) jar salsa
1   (15.5-ounce) can black beans, rinsed and drained
1   (11-ounce) can corn kernels, drained
1   large tomato, coarsely chopped
2   tablespoons fresh lime juice
2   cloves garlic, minced
2   tablespoons chopped fresh cilantro
½   teaspoon ground cumin

Combine all ingredients in a medium-size bowl. Cover and chill 30 minutes before serving.

Yield: 6 cups.

Note: When large tomatoes are too pale or lack flavor you can substitute 3 Roma tomatoes.

Per (¼ cup) serving: 35 calories, 0.2 g. fat, 0 mg. cholesterol, 159 mg. sodium

Cranberry Salsa

1 (10-ounce) package fresh or frozen
   whole cranberries
2 oranges, peeled, seeded, and quartered
1 jalapeño pepper, chopped
½ cup sugar
½ cup coarsely chopped red onion
½ cup chopped pecans
¼ cup loosely packed fresh cilantro

Place ingredients in bowl of food processor.
Pulse 4 or 5 times until mixture is coarsely
chopped.

Yield: 3 cups.

*Per (¼ cup) serving: 87 calories, 3.2 g. fat, 0 mg.
cholesterol, 1 mg. sodium*

This zesty relish
pairs wonderfully
with turkey. For a
festive holiday salsa,
try it with sweet
potato or tortilla
chips.

Pineapple Salsa

½ medium-size fresh pineapple, trimmed
  and coarsely chopped
1 red bell pepper, chopped
1 jalapeño pepper, seeded and chopped
4 green onions, thinly sliced
¼ cup finely chopped red onion,
2 tablespoons chopped fresh cilantro
2 tablespoons fresh lime juice

Combine ingredients; cover and chill.

Yield: 4½ cups

Note: For a zesty fruit salad, chop the remaining half of the pineapple, and add it to the salsa.

Per (¼ cup) serving: 21 calories, 0.1 g. fat, 0 mg. cholesterol, 6 mg. sodium

For ease, look for trimmed or precut fresh pineapple in the produce section of large supermarkets.

Super-Simple Snack Mix

 kid friendly

⅔ cup slivered almonds
3 cups low-fat granola cereal with raisins
1 cup corn-and-rice cereal squares
1 cup oatmeal squares cereal
1 cup semisweet chocolate mini-morsels
⅔ cup (3 ounces) dried cherries or cranberries

Preheat oven to 350°.

Place almonds on baking sheet, and bake 5 to 7 minutes or until lightly toasted; cool.

Combine cereals, morsels, dried cherries, and almonds; stirring well. Store in an airtight container.

Yield: 6½ cups.

For a "melt-free" hiking or camping snack, you can substitute candy-coated mini-morsels.

Cajun Seasoning Blend

3 tablespoons paprika
2 tablespoons ground red pepper
2 tablespoons salt
1 tablespoon garlic powder
1 tablespoon dried thyme
1 tablespoon dried basil
2 teaspoons onion powder
2 teaspoons black pepper
1 teaspoon crushed red pepper

Combine all ingredients; store in an airtight container.

Yield: ⅔ cup.

This flavorful blend can be used for classic Louisiana dishes or tossed into boiling water to season shrimp.

Mexican Seasoning Blend

¼ cup chili powder
3 tablespoons ground cumin
1 tablespoon garlic powder
½-1 tablespoon ground black pepper
1 tablespoon salt
1 teaspoon cayenne pepper

Combine all ingredients; store in an airtight container.

Yield: ½ cup.

This zesty seasoning can substitute for packaged taco seasoning mix, but it also doubles as a dry spice rub for grilled meats. Or, stir it into sour cream for a quick dip.

Index

184   Index

S

About the Authors

Susan Dosier, a North Carolina native, is a former Foods Editor for *Southern Living* magazine. Today, as President of the Susan Dosier Co., she plans food events, writes, and travels the country speaking on food trends and entertaining creatively at home. Her clients have included *Cooking Light* and *Progressive Farmer* magazines, Healthy Choice foods, and the North Carolina Department of Agriculture. Susan and her husband, Des Keller, live in Birmingham with two busy toddlers, Lucy Lynn and Frances Ann.

Julia Dowling Rutland began her culinary career as a chef's apprentice in her hometown of Birmingham and landed a spot at *Southern Living* as a Test Kitchens Home Economist. After working as a Publishing and Marketing Consultant for The Wimmer Companies, Julia runs her home-based company, **Plate 2 Plate.** Her activities include developing and testing recipes, cookbook editing, cooking demonstrations, and food and kitchen lectures. Julia and her husband, Dit, live in Memphis with their very busy toddler, Emily.

About the Illustrator

Robin Richards has worked as a graphic designer and illustrator for 15 years with clients such as Oxmoor House book publishers, Marcel Schurman greeting cards and Birmingham Children's Theatre. She recently began painting professionally and is known for her vivid use of color and her creative whimsy. Robin brings that same cheerful energy to raising her two daughters, Georgia and Sarah. Robin and her husband Courtland live in Daphne, Alabama.